BRINCANDO COM INGLÊS

WORKBOOK

1

**ENSINO FUNDAMENTAL
ANOS INICIAIS**

RENATO MENDES CURTO JÚNIOR
ANNA CAROLINA GUIMARÃES
CIBELE MENDES

Editora do Brasil

CONTENTS

UNIT 1
FUN TIMES WITH FRIENDS _____ 3

UNIT 2
I LOVE PETS _____ 6

UNIT 3
A SPECIAL PLACE, THE SCHOOL! _____ 9

UNIT 4
MY FAVORITE FOOD _____ 12

UNIT 5
SUMMER VACATION _____ 15

UNIT 6
OUR FAMILY _____ 19

UNIT 7
HOME SWEET HOME _____ 23

UNIT 8
MY CLOTHES _____ 29

UNIT 1
FUN TIMES WITH FRIENDS

1 WHAT ARE THEY SAYING?

GOOD MORNING.   •   GOOD AFTERNOON
GOOD EVENING.   •   GOOD NIGHT.

A) _____

B) _____

C) _____

D) _____

2 COMPLETE WITH **I** OR **YOU**.

A) _____ LIKE PASTA.

B) _____ PREFER STEAK AND VEGETABLE SALAD.

C) _____ LIKE FRUIT SALAD.

D) _____ LIKE ICE CREAM AND CAKE.

3 COMPLETE THE SENTENCE.

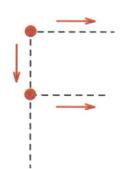

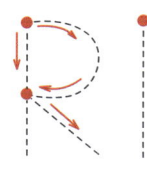

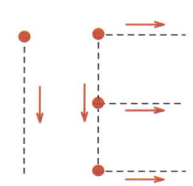

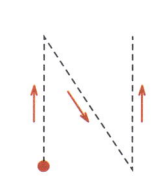

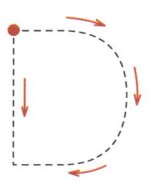

THEY ARE F R I E N D S

4 CLASS SURVEY. WALK AROUND THE CLASS AND ASK WHICH OF THESE ACTIVITIES YOUR CLASSMATES LIKE. WRITE THEIR NAMES IN THE TABLE.

EXAMPLE

— DO YOU LIKE DANCING?

— YES, I DO. / NO, I DON'T.

FIND TWO CLASSMATES WHO LIKE:	NAME	NAME
DANCING	PEDRO	ALINE
A) WATCHING CARTOONS		
B) PLAYING VIDEO GAMES		
C) PLAYING WITH BUILDING-BLOCK TOYS		
D) WATCHING SOCCER MATCHES		
E) RIDING A BIKE		
F) PLAYING BOARD GAMES		

UNIT 2
I LOVE PETS

1 MATCH THE ANIMAL NAMES TO THEIR PICTURES.

A) TURTLE

B) BIRD

C) DOG

D) HAMSTER

E) RABBIT

F) CAT

2 WHAT ARE THEY? COMPLETE THEIR NAMES WITH THE MISSING VOWELS.

A) D___G

B) R___BB___T

C) G___ ___N___ ___ P___G

D) H___MST___R

E) B___RD

F) T___RTL___

3 COLOR THE PICTURES ACCORDING TO THE INSTRUCTIONS.

🔵 DOG   🟢 RABBIT

🔴 BIRD   🟡 GUINEA PIG

UNIT 3
A SPECIAL PLACE, THE SCHOOL!

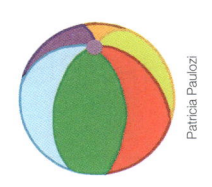

1 COMPLETE WITH THE INITIAL LETTER OF THE WORDS.

A) ____PPLE

B) ____ALL

C) ____AT

D) ____OLL

E) ____UN

F) ____CE CREAM

G) ____RANGE

H) ____ILK

2 COUNT AND WRITE THE NUMBER OF ITEMS IN EACH GROUP.

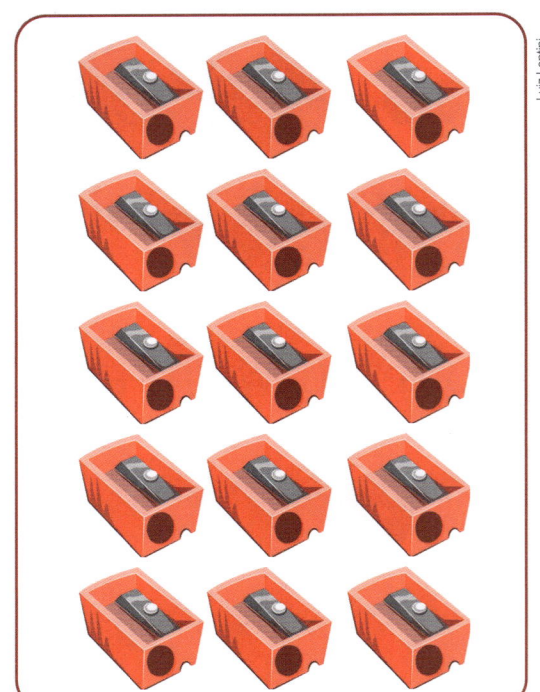

A)

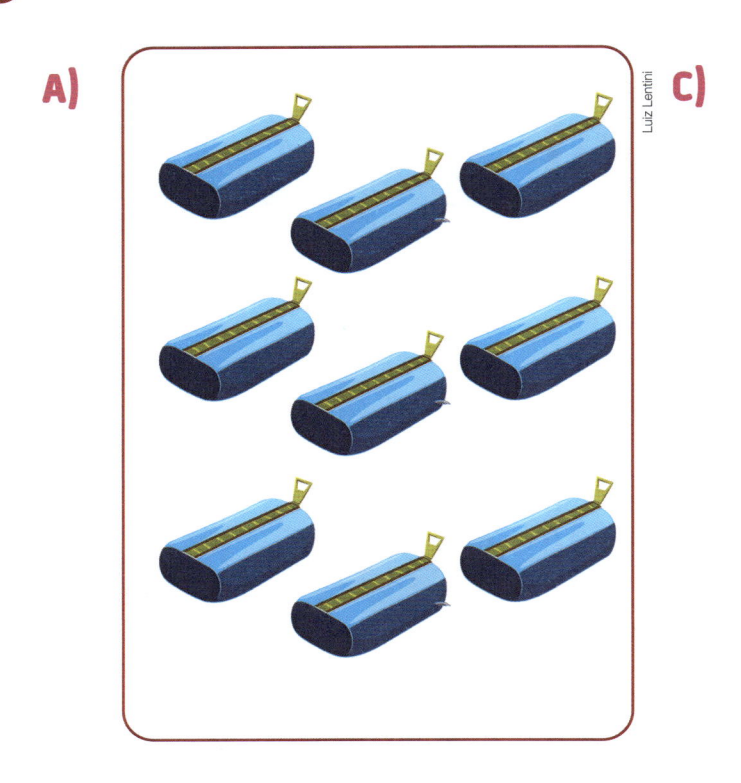

_____ PENCIL CASES.

B)

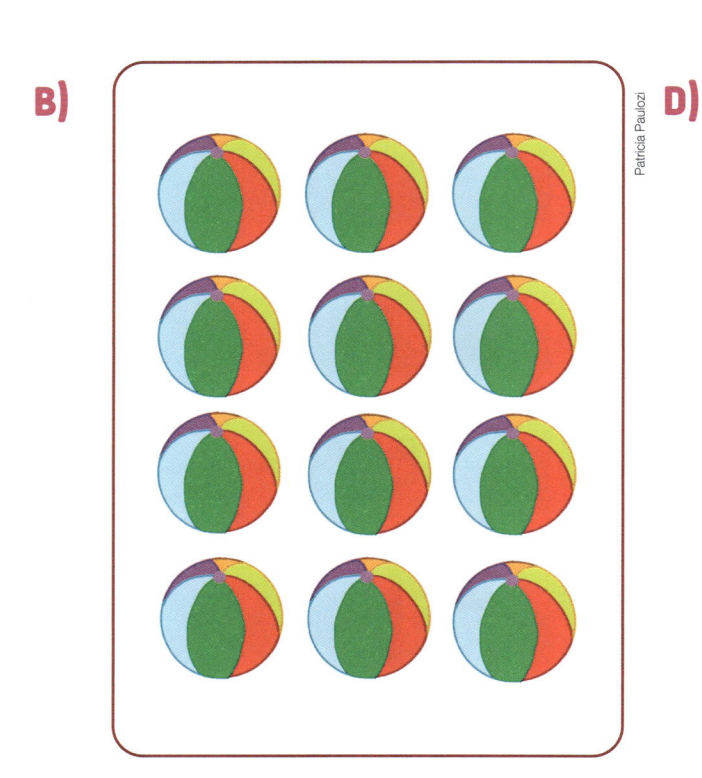

_____ BALLS.

C)

_____ SHARPENERS.

D)

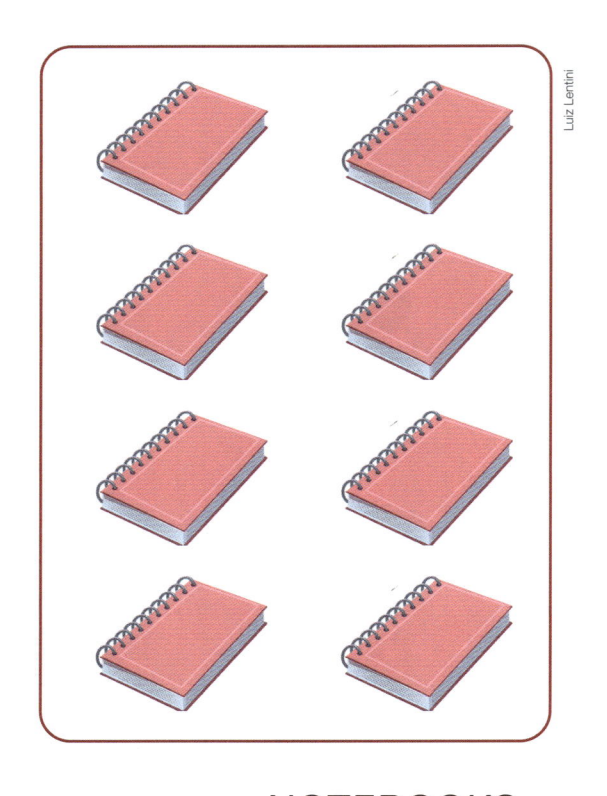

_____ NOTEBOOKS.

3 FIND, COLOR, AND COUNT THESE SCHOOL OBJECTS IN THE IMAGE.

- ☐ PENCIL
- ☐ NOTEBOOK
- ☐ PEN
- ☐ ERASER
- ☐ RULER
- ☐ BOOK

NOW, TRACE THE WORD.

SCHOOL

UNIT 4
MY FAVORITE FOOD

1 CIRCLE THE FOOD YOU EAT AT BREAKFAST.

FRUIT SALAD

SANDWICH

BREAD

SALAD

BEANS

CEREAL

2 WRITE THE NAMES OF THE FOODS AND FIND THEM IN THE WORD SEARCH.

A) _____

B) _____

C) _____

D) _____

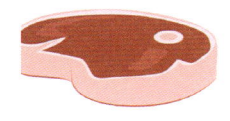

E) _____

F) _____

G) _____

H) _____

W	B	R	E	A	D	A	S	G	J	R	I	C	E	I
F	R	K	H	A	M	B	U	R	G	E	R	O	P	D
T	H	R	G	J	T	Q	X	K	I	E	W	D	Q	G
G	I	N	U	C	H	I	C	K	E	N	K	G	E	W
J	Y	L	W	Y	U	M	D	Q	A	X	E	F	I	E
C	A	K	E	R	T	B	Y	J	P	A	S	T	A	Q
F	P	Y	A	G	J	K	P	E	I	Y	Q	S	D	R
K	L	G	F	I	S	H	U	R	W	V	M	E	A	T

THIRTEEN 13

3 COLOR YOUR FAVORITE FOODS AND DRINKS.

4 WORK IN PAIRS. SHOW YOUR PICTURES TO YOUR CLASSMATE AND TALK ABOUT YOUR PREFERENCES.

EXAMPLE

— WHAT IS YOUR FAVORITE FOOD?

— I LIKE PIZZA.

— WHAT IS YOUR FAVORITE DRINK?

— I LIKE JUICE.

5 NOW TALK TO YOUR CLASSMATE ABOUT THE FOODS AND THE DRINKS YOU DISLIKE.

EXAMPLE

— I DISLIKE ONION. AND I DISLIKE MILK.

UNIT 5
SUMMER VACATION

1 DRAW A SCENE WITH:

- A BOAT
- A PARASOL
- A BUCKET
- A SHOVEL
- THE SUN
- SAND
- SEA

2 WHAT IS THIS? NAME IT CORRECTLY.

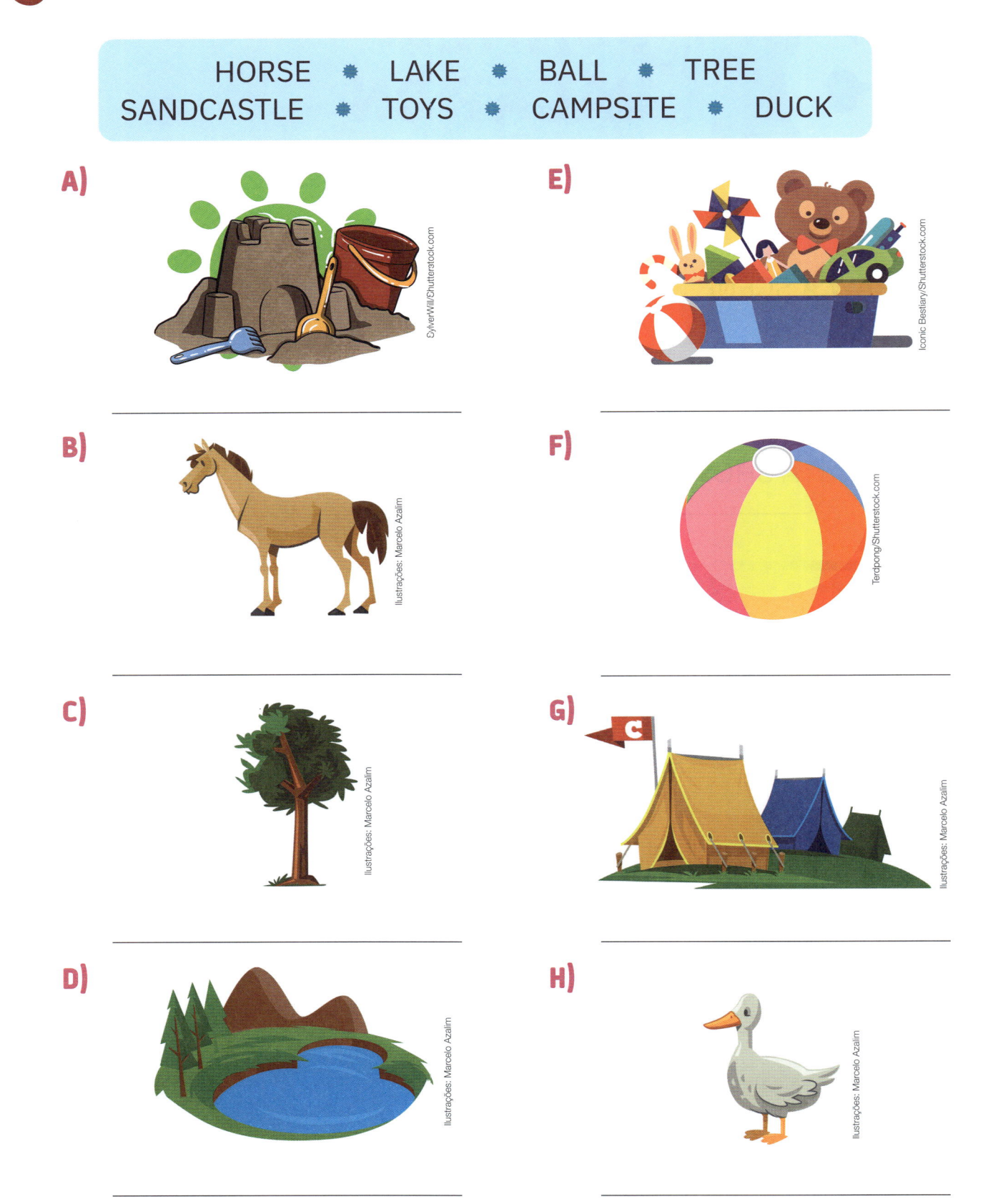

> HORSE • LAKE • BALL • TREE
> SANDCASTLE • TOYS • CAMPSITE • DUCK

A) _____

B) _____

C) _____

D) _____

E) _____

F) _____

G) _____

H) _____

3 WRITE THE MISSING LETTER TO COMPLETE THE WORDS.
IT'S VACATION TIME! LET'S GO TO...

A) THE BE____CH

C) THE P____RK

B) THE C____UNTRYSIDE

D) THE CAMPS____TE

E) THE S____A

4 COLOR THE ACTIVITIES THAT WE CAN DO AT A PARK.

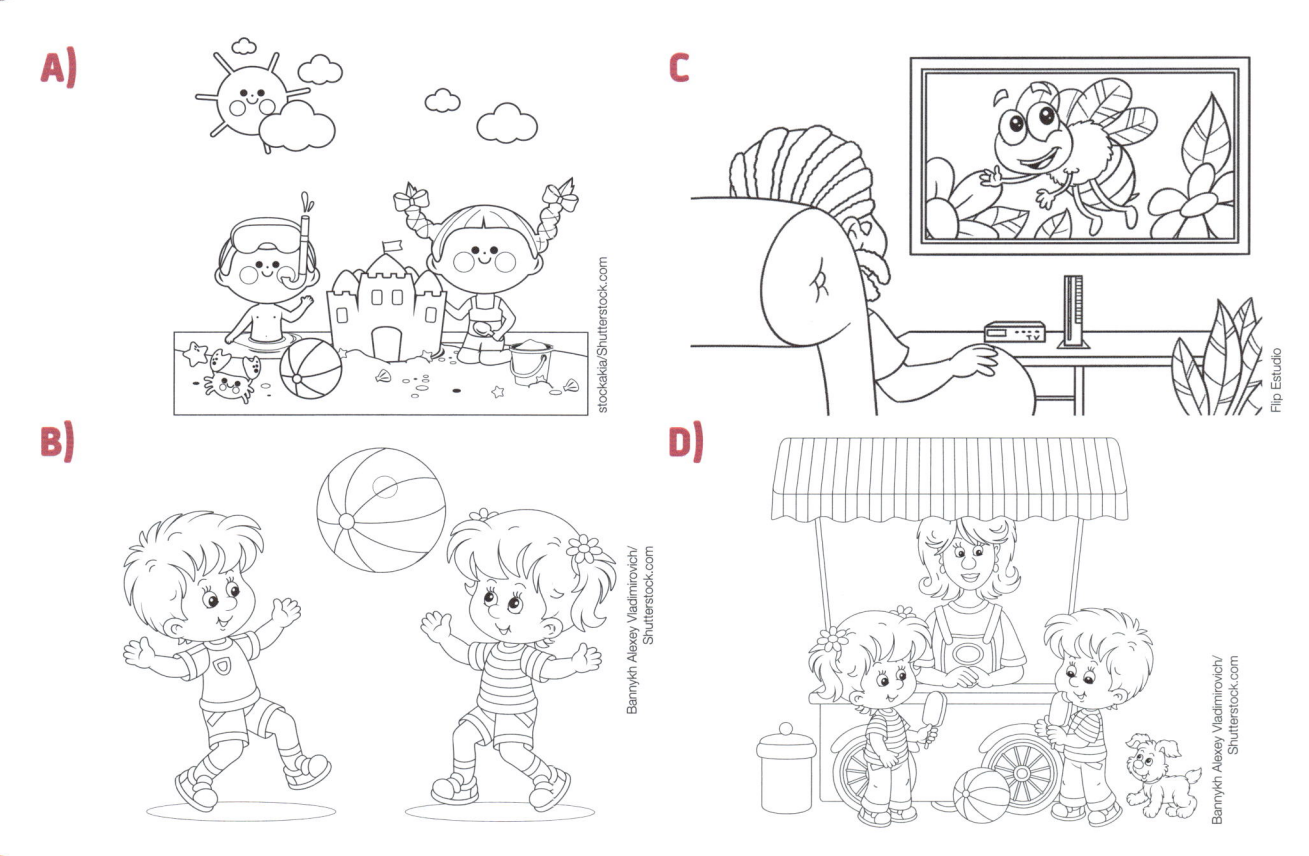

A)

B)

C)

D)

5 MATCH THE NAMES WITH THE PICTURES.

PLAY BALL

RIDE A BIKE

MAKE A SANDCASTLE

JUMP ROPE

UNIT 6 OUR FAMILY

1 WHO ARE THEY?

MOTHER * GRANDMOTHER * BROTHER * GRANDFATHER
SISTER * AUNT * FATHER * COUSIN * UNCLE

1. _____
2. _____
3. _____
4. _____
5. _____
6. _____
7. _____
8. _____
9. _____

NINETEEN 19

2 COMPLETE CYNTHIA'S SENTENCES WITH THE PRONOUNS **THEY, HE, SHE, IT, WE, YOU**.

HI. I AM CYNTHIA.

THIS IS THIAGO. ____ IS MY BROTHER.

THIS IS SYLVIA. ____ IS MY BEST FRIEND.

____ STUDY AT MLK ELEMENTARY SCHOOL.

THIS IS MLK SCHOOL. ____ IS REALLY BIG.

____ ARE OUR TEACHERS: MS. MOURA AND MS. JONES.

WHAT ABOUT ____? IS YOUR SCHOOL BIG?

3 FIND THE FAMILY MEMBERS AND CIRCLE THEM.

MOTHER • GRANDMOTHER • BROTHER • GRANDFATHER
SISTER • AUNT • FATHER • COUSIN • UNCLE

```
Q U T F A T H E R F B E J W I
B L U T D Q G Z R S K E C H Q
Q U I G R A N D F A T H E R L
C O U S I N V I F H Q S I F L
Q B T Y G A D Y Z G P Z Y Z B
M U N C L E D U J M O T H E R
F P Y A G J K P E I Y Q S D R
K L G H I H H U R W V V A A X
K E U H D J B E I E A K O M D
G R A N D M O T H E R O R X F
N E H S T H Y C I Z E A U N T
Z H R S I S T E R E T R K E S
O W H D X E R B R O T H E R B
```

4 LOOK AT LANA'S FAMILY PHOTO.

NOW DRAW YOUR FAMILY.

UNIT 7
HOME SWEET HOME

1 WHICH PART OF THE HOUSE IS IT?

A) 
- ☐ BEDROOM
- ☐ KITCHEN
- ☐ LIVING ROOM
- ☐ BATHROOM

B)
- ☐ BEDROOM
- ☐ KITCHEN
- ☐ LIVING ROOM
- ☐ BATHROOM

2 COLOR THE PICTURES ACCORDING TO THE INSTRUCTIONS.

- 🔴 WINDOW
- 🟡 DOOR
- 🔵 ROOF
- 🟢 WALL

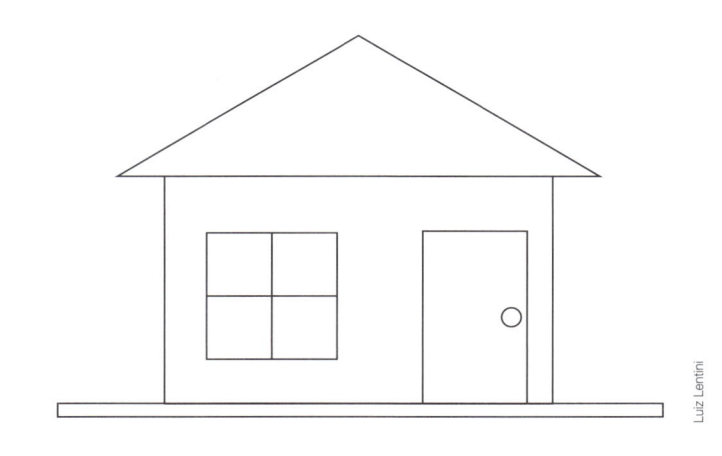

TWENTY-THREE 23

3 MATCH THE NAMES TO THE IMAGES.

A) SQUARE

B) TRIANGLE

C) RECTANGLE

D) CIRCLE

4 WHAT IS THE CORRECT NAME?

A)

- [ ] SOFA
- [ ] STOVE

B)

- [ ] SHOWER
- [ ] REFRIGERATOR

C)

- [ ] SINK
- [ ] STOVE

D)

- [ ] TOILET SEAT
- [ ] CUPBOARD

5 LOOK AT THIS BIRTHDAY PARTY INVITATION. MATCH THE COLUMNS.

BÁRBARA

6 YEARS OLD PARTY

SATURDAY 3:00 SPORTS CLUB

WHO?   SATURDAY

HOW OLD?   SPORTS CLUB

WHERE?   BÁRBARA

WHEN?   6 YEARS OLD

6 IMAGINE YOU ARE TALKING TO PEDRO. MATCH THE QUESTIONS TO THE ANSWERS.

WHO ARE YOU?   SHE IS MY SISTER

WHERE ARE YOU?   I'M PEDRO.

WHAT IS THIS?   IT'S MY NEW PHONE.

WHO IS SHE?   I'M AT SCHOOL.

7 COMPLETE THE WORDS WITH THE MISSING LETTERS.

W____O IS HE?

HE IS JOHNNY.

WH____RE IS SHE?

SHE IS AT SCHOOL.

WHA____ IS THIS?

IT IS A BOOK.

UNIT 8
MY CLOTHES

1 COLOR THE ITEMS ACCORDING TO THE INSTRUCTIONS.

🟠 FEET   🟡 ARMS   🟢 LEGS

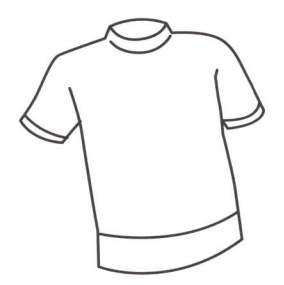

2 WHAT ARE THEY? FOLLOW THE EXAMPLES.

A) IT IS A PAIR OF PANTS.

E) IT IS A T-SHIRT.

B)

F)

C)

G)

D)

H)

3 CIRCLE THE ITEMS YOU WEAR ON YOUR FEET.

4 CIRCLE THE ITEMS YOU WEAR ON YOUR HEAD.

5 COLOR JO'S CLOTHES.

THE DRESS IS RED.

THE T-SHIRT IS BLUE.

THE PAJAMAS ARE BROWN.

THE SOCKS ARE GREY.

THE COAT IS PINK.

THE SKIRT IS YELLOW.

BRINCANDO COM INGLÊS

1

ENSINO FUNDAMENTAL
ANOS INICIAIS

RENATO MENDES CURTO JÚNIOR

Licenciado em Letras

Certificado de proficiência em Língua Inglesa pela Universidade de Michigan e TOEFL

Autor de livros de educação a distância

Professor de Língua Inglesa e Portuguesa na rede particular de ensino desde 1986

ANNA CAROLINA GUIMARÃES

Licenciada em pedagogia

Especialista em Educação Infantil e anos iniciais

Especialista em neuropsicopedagogia

Coordenadora pedagógica de Educação básica

CIBELE MENDES

Mestre em Educação

Licenciada em Pedagogia

Certificado de proficiência em Língua Inglesa pela Fluency Academy

Coordenadora pedagógica de Educação Infantil aos Anos Finais do Ensino Fundamental

Editora do Brasil

Dados Internacionais de Catalogação na Publicação (CIP)
(Câmara Brasileira do Livro, SP, Brasil)

Curto Júnior, Renato Mendes
  Brincando com inglês 1 : ensino fundamental : anos iniciais / Renato Mendes Curto Júnior, Anna Carolina Guimarães, Cibele Mendes. -- 5. ed. -- São Paulo : Editora do Brasil, 2024. -- (Brincando com)

  ISBN 978-85-10-09503-7 (aluno)
  ISBN 978-85-10-09504-4 (professor)

  1. Língua inglesa (Ensino fundamental)
I. Guimarães, Anna Carolina. II. Mendes, Cibele.
III. Título. IV. Série.

24-193768   CDD-372.652

Índices para catálogo sistemático:

  1. Língua inglesa : Ensino fundamental 372.652
  Eliane de Freitas Leite - Bibliotecária - CRB 8/8415

© Editora do Brasil S.A., 2024
Todos os direitos reservados

Direção-geral: Paulo Serino de Souza

Diretoria editorial: Felipe Ramos Poletti
Gerência editorial de conteúdo didático: Erika Caldin
Gerência editorial de produção e design: Ulisses Pires
Supervisão de design: Aurélio Gadini Camilo
Supervisão de arte: Abdonildo José de Lima Santos
Supervisão de revisão: Elaine Silva
Supervisão de iconografia: Léo Burgos
Supervisão de digital: Priscila Hernandez
Supervisão de controle e planejamento editorial: Roseli Said
Supervisão de direitos autorais: Jennifer Xavier

Supervisão editorial: Carla Felix Lopes e Diego Mata
Edição: Graziele Arantes Mattiuzzi, Sheila Fabre, Natália Feulo, Danuza D. Gonçalves e Nayra Simões
Assistência editorial: Igor Gonçalves, Julia do Nascimento e Pedro Andrade Bezerra
Revisão: 2014 Soluções Editoriais, Alexander Siqueira, Andréia Andrade, Beatriz Dorini, Gabriel Ornelas, Giovana Sanches, Jonathan Busato, Júlia Castelo Branco, Maisa Akazawa, Mariana Paixão, Martin Gonçalves, Rita Costa, Rosani Andreani e Sandra Fernandes
Pesquisa iconográfica: Maria Santos e Selma Nagano
Tratamento de imagens: Robson Mereu
Projeto gráfico: Caronte Design
Capa: Caronte Design
Imagem de capa: Thais Castro
Edição de arte: Camila de Camargo e Marcos Gubiotti
Ilustrações: Dayane Raven, Desenhorama, DKO Estúdio, Luiz Lentini, Marcelo Azalim, Reinaldo Rosa e Vanessa Alexandre
Editoração eletrônica: Abel Design
Licenciamentos de textos: Cinthya Utiyama, Jennifer Xavier, Paula Harue Tozaki e Renata Garbellini
Controle e planejamento editorial: Ana Paula Barbosa, Bianca Gomes, Juliana Gonçalves, Maria Trofino, Terezinha Oliveira e Valéria Alves

5ª edição / 1ª impressão, 2024
Impresso na Hawaii Gráfica e Editora

Editora do Brasil
Avenida das Nações Unidas, 12901
Torre Oeste, 20º andar
São Paulo, SP – CEP: 04578-910
Fone: + 55 11 3226-0211
www.editoradobrasil.com.br

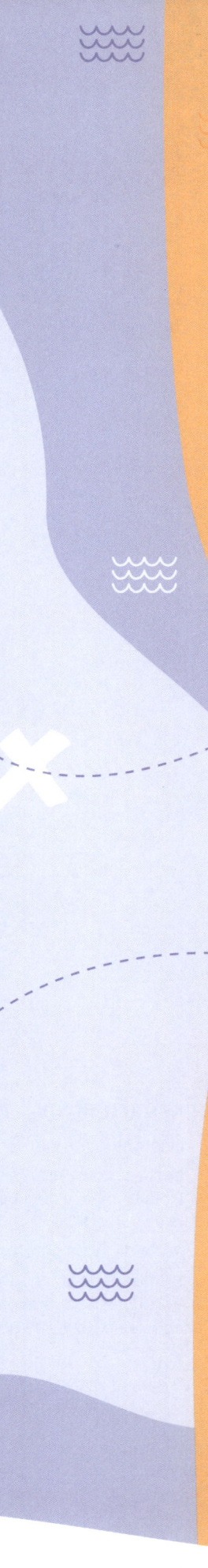

abdr
ASSOCIAÇÃO BRASILEIRA DOS DIREITOS REPROGRÁFICOS
Respeite o direito autoral

CONTEÚDO DIGITAL PARA ALUNOS
Cadastre-se e transforme seus estudos em uma experiência única de aprendizado:

1

Entre na página de cadastro:
https://sistemas.editoradobrasil.com.br/cadastro

2

Além dos seus dados pessoais e dos dados de sua escola, adicione ao cadastro o código do aluno, que garantirá a exclusividade do seu ingresso à plataforma.

2164188A6698832

3

Depois, acesse:
https://leb.editoradobrasil.com.br/
e navegue pelos conteúdos digitais de sua coleção **:D**

Lembre-se de que esse código, pessoal e intransferível, é valido por um ano. Guarde-o com cuidado, pois é a única maneira de você acessar os conteúdos da plataforma.

Editora do Brasil

APRESENTAÇÃO

QUERIDO ALUNO, QUERIDA ALUNA,

ESTE MATERIAL FOI ELABORADO PARA QUE VOCÊ APRENDA INGLÊS DE FORMA DIVERTIDA, POR MEIO DE ATIVIDADES ESTIMULANTES E DESAFIADORAS, COM O INTUITO DE TRANSFORMAR A SALA DE AULA EM UM ESPAÇO PARA PRATICAR A LÍNGUA INGLESA BRINCANDO!

NESTA NOVA VERSÃO DO **BRINCANDO COM INGLÊS**, CADA AULA SERÁ UMA NOVA EXPERIÊNCIA, E VOCÊ NÃO VAI QUERER PARAR DE APRENDER. VAMOS COMEÇAR?

OS AUTORES

CONHEÇA SEU LIVRO

BOAS-VINDAS À NOVA EDIÇÃO DO BRINCANDO COM INGLÊS!

LET'S START!
NO INÍCIO DE CADA VOLUME, ESTA SEÇÃO RESGATA CONHECIMENTOS PRÉVIOS E APRESENTA ATIVIDADES LÚDICAS QUE POSSIBILITAM A PREPARAÇÃO PARA OS NOVOS CONTEÚDOS.

COMPREHENSION
AS ATIVIDADES DESTA SEÇÃO VISAM À COMPREENSÃO DO TEXTO VISTO NA ABERTURA DE UNIDADE.

VOCABULARY
APRESENTA O VOCABULÁRIO DAS PALAVRAS VISTAS NA UNIDADE, COM A TRADUÇÃO EM LÍNGUA PORTUGUESA.

LET'S PLAY
SEÇÃO RELACIONADA AOS CONCEITOS PROPOSTOS E À TEMÁTICA DA UNIDADE. VOCÊ ENCONTRARÁ ATIVIDADES LÚDICAS, COMO DIAGRAMA DE PALAVRAS, JOGOS DE RELACIONAR, JOGOS DE ERROS, DESAFIOS ETC.

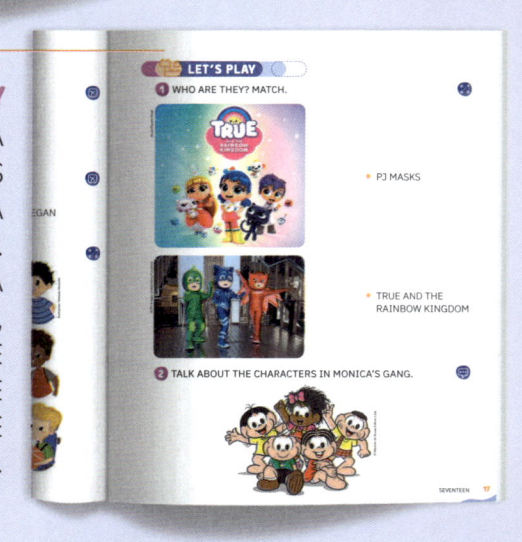

LET'S LISTEN
SEÇÃO COM ATIVIDADES QUE TÊM COMO OBJETIVO A COMPREENSÃO DE ÁUDIOS.

LET'S HAVE FUN
LOCALIZADA NO FINAL DAS UNIDADES, CONTÉM ATIVIDADES VARIADAS CUJA PROPOSTA É DESENVOLVER O ESTUDO DA LÍNGUA INGLESA COM ATIVIDADES PRÁTICAS, AMPLIANDO O CONHECIMENTO E O VOCABULÁRIO TRABALHADO.

GOOD DEED
APRESENTA ATIVIDADES TEMÁTICAS DE CUNHO SOCIAL E ÉTICO RELACIONADAS AO ASSUNTO DE CADA UNIDADE. ABORDA AS COMPETÊNCIAS GERAIS E SOCIOEMOCIONAIS DA BNCC E AS ATIVIDADES FEITAS EM GRUPOS OU DUPLAS.

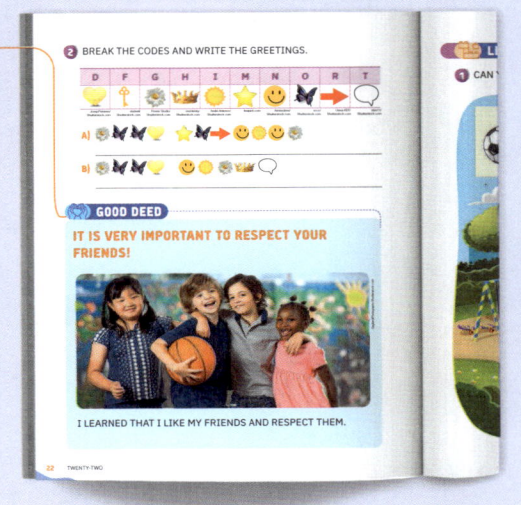

AFTER THIS UNIT I CAN
SEÇÃO DE AUTOAVALIAÇÃO E ACOMPANHAMENTO PROCESSUAL PELO ALUNO E PELO PROFESSOR.

ENGLISH AROUND THE WORLD
SEÇÃO QUE CONTEMPLA A DIMENSÃO INTERCULTURAL DA LÍNGUA INGLESA, TRABALHANDO ELEMENTOS DA CULTURA EM QUE SE FALA O IDIOMA COMO LÍNGUA OFICIAL OU FRANCA. TAMBÉM SÃO ESTUDADOS OS ASPECTOS INTERCULTURAIS DE OUTROS PAÍSES.

GRAMMAR POINT
BOXE COM CONTEÚDOS GRAMATICAIS PARA QUE VOCÊ COMPREENDA A ESTRUTURA ESTUDADA E SISTEMATIZE ESCRITA E ORALIDADE.

DIGITAL PLAY

SEÇÃO QUE TRABALHA ATIVIDADES COM USO DE TECNOLOGIA: FILMAGEM, FOTOS, USO DE APPS E JOGOS *ON-LINE*.

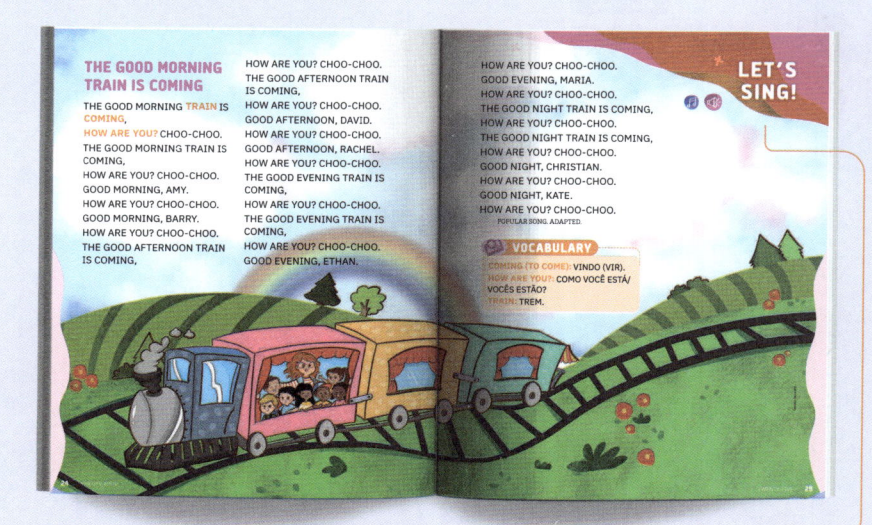

CELEBRATIONS

ENCARTES COM ATIVIDADES RELACIONADAS A DATAS COMEMORATIVAS.

LET'S SING!

MÚSICAS PARA OS ALUNOS CANTAREM E PRATICAREM O VOCABULÁRIO VISTO NA UNIDADE DE FORMA LÚDICA E DIVERTIDA.

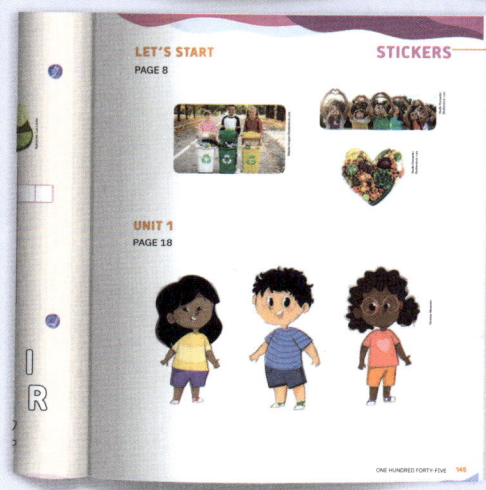

STICKERS

ADESIVOS PARA COLAR EM ALGUMAS ATIVIDADES.

ÍCONES

- ADESIVO
- APONTAR
- CANTAR
- CARTONADO
- CIRCULAR
- COLAR
- COLORIR
- CONTAR
- DESENHAR
- ENCONTRAR/PESQUISAR
- FALAR OU CONVERSAR
- LIGAR/RELACIONAR
- MARCAR
- RECORTAR
- TRAÇAR/ESCREVER

CONTENTS

LET'S START! — 8

UNIT 1
FUN TIMES WITH FRIENDS — 15

UNIT 2
I LOVE PETS — 27

UNIT 3
A SPECIAL PLACE, THE SCHOOL! — 36

UNIT 4
MY FAVORITE FOOD — 48

UNIT 5
SUMMER VACATION — 58

UNIT 6
OUR FAMILY — 69

UNIT 7
HOME SWEET HOME — 81

UNIT 8
MY CLOTHES — 94

REVIEW — 107

PICTURE DICTIONARY — 118

INDEX — 127

  SONGS — 127

  LISTENINGS — 127

CELEBRATIONS — 129

STICKERS — 145

LET'S START!

1 LOOK AT THE PICTURE. PASTE THE STICKERS AND COLOR THE WORDS.

LOVE
PEACE
HEALTH
RECYCLING

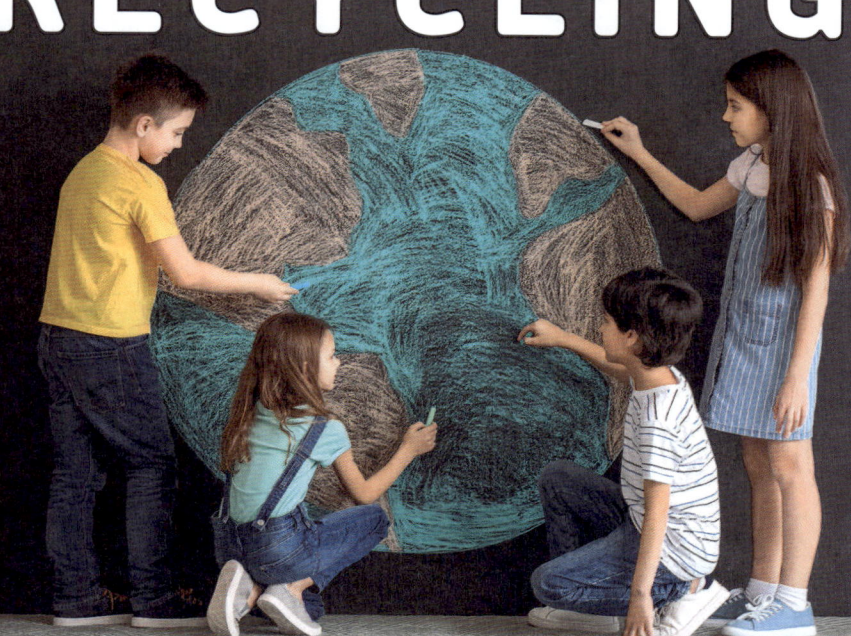

2 FIND AND CIRCLE THE SEA ANIMALS.

3 FIND THE WAY AND TRACE THE WORDS.

SHARK

FISH

4 HOW MANY? LOOK AND COUNT THE HAPPY FACES.

5 CHECK THE CORRECT ACTIONS.

A) ☐

B) ☐

C) ☐

D) ☐

6 CHECK THE HEALTHY FOODS. THEN TRACE THE WORDS.

A) ☐

FRENCH FRIES

B) ☐

VEGETABLES

7 CIRCLE THE HAPPY GIRL. THEN TRACE THE WORDS.

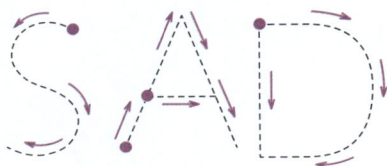

HAPPY   SAD

8 POINT AT THE SCHOOL OBJECTS. THEN MATCH THEM WITH THEIR NAMES.

BACKPACK   PENCIL CASE   BOOK   PENCIL

9 IDENTIFY THE CHARACTERS. USE:

🟠 ORANGE FOR GIRLS

🟢 GREEN FOR BOYS

14 FOURTEEN

UNIT 1
FUN TIMES WITH FRIENDS

GOOD MORNING, TERRY. **WHAT'S UP? MY NAME** IS JOHNNY.

NICE TO MEET YOU, TERRY. I'M ANNE.

HI, TERRY! I'M DAVID.

HI, TERRY. **I'M** KATE. THESE ARE MY **FRIENDS**.

GOOD MORNING! I'M TOM. DO YOU LIKE TO **PLAY**?

HELLO! MY NAME IS TERRY.

MY NAME IS MEGAN. I NEED TO **GO HOME**. **BYE**!

VOCABULARY

BYE: TCHAU.
FRIENDS: AMIGOS.
GANG: TURMA.
GO HOME: IR PARA CASA.
HAPPY: FELIZ.
I AM (I'M): EU SOU.
MY NAME: MEU NOME.
NICE TO MEET YOU: PRAZER EM CONHECÊ-LO.
PLAY: BRINCAR.
WHAT'S UP?: COMO VAI? / COMO ESTÁ?

COMPREHENSION

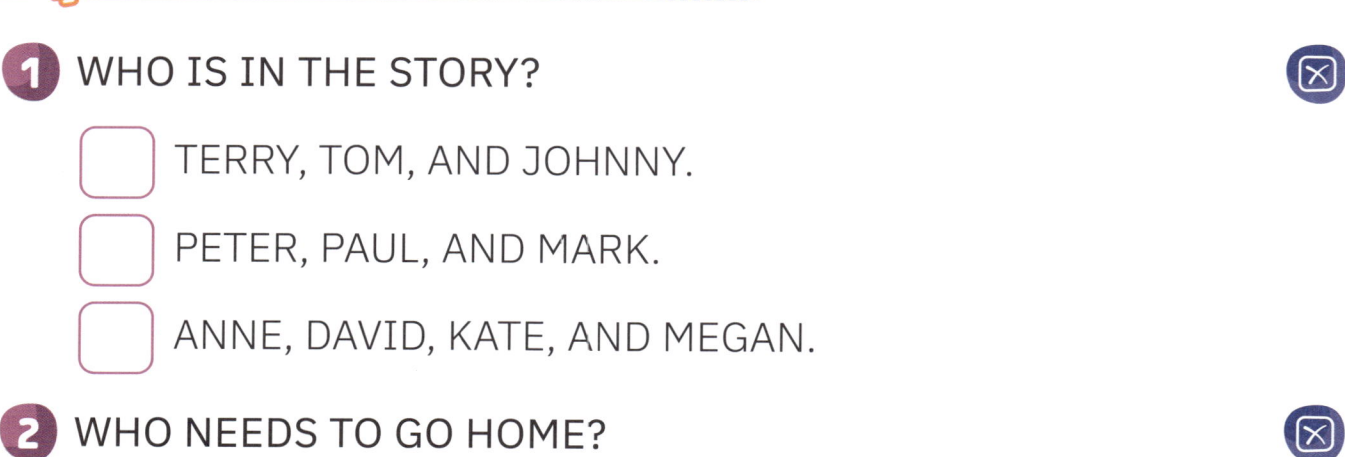

1 WHO IS IN THE STORY?

☐ TERRY, TOM, AND JOHNNY.

☐ PETER, PAUL, AND MARK.

☐ ANNE, DAVID, KATE, AND MEGAN.

2 WHO NEEDS TO GO HOME?

☐ KATE   ☐ MEGAN

3 MATCH THE FRIENDS.

LET'S PLAY

1 WHO ARE THEY? MATCH.

- PJ MASKS

- TRUE AND THE RAINBOW KINGDOM

2 TALK ABOUT THE CHARACTERS IN MONICA'S GANG.

SEVENTEEN 17

3 WHOSE SHADOWS ARE THESE? PLACE THE STICKERS AND WRITE **BOY** OR **GIRL**.

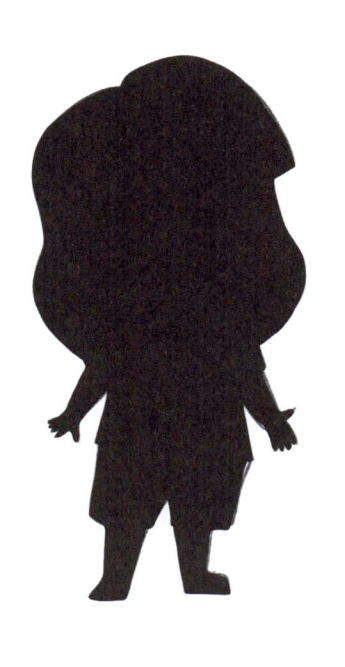

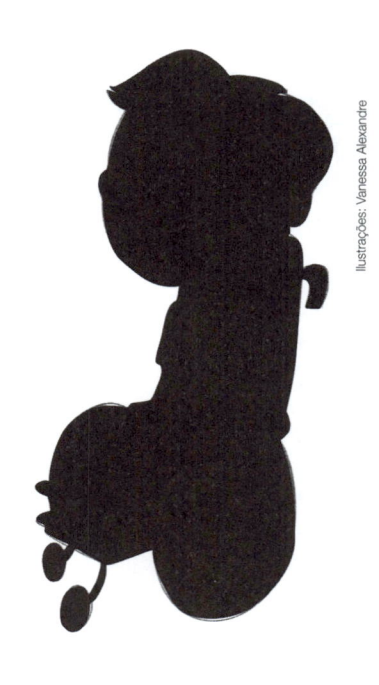

ENGLISH AROUND THE WORLD

GREETINGS AROUND THE WORLD

INFORMAL

- HEY!
- MORNING!
- SUP?

FORMAL

- GOOD MORNING!
- GOOD TO SEE YOU!
- NICE TO MEET YOU!

DIGITAL PLAY

MY GANG

TAKE A SELFIE WITH YOUR FRIENDS.

LET'S PLAY

1 WHAT DO THEY LIKE TO PLAY? MATCH.

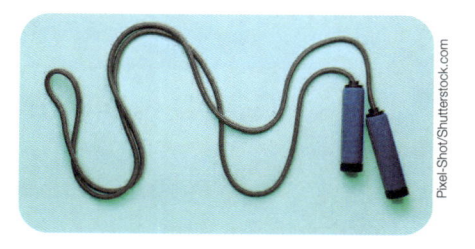

A) I LIKE SKATEBOARDS!

B) I LIKE BIKES!

C) I LIKE BALLS!

D) I LIKE TAG!

E) I LIKE BLIND MAN'S BUFF!

F) I LIKE JUMP ROPES!

LET'S LISTEN

1 WHAT ARE THEY SAYING? LISTEN AND NUMBER.

A)  ☐ GOOD NIGHT.

C)  ☐ GOOD AFTERNOON.

B)  ☐ GOOD EVENING.

D)  ☐ GOOD MORNING.

VOCABULARY

GOOD AFTERNOON: BOA TARDE.
GOOD EVENING: BOA NOITE.
GOOD MORNING: BOM DIA.
GOOD NIGHT: BOA NOITE.

LET'S PLAY

1 WRITE THE CORRECT GREETING.

A)

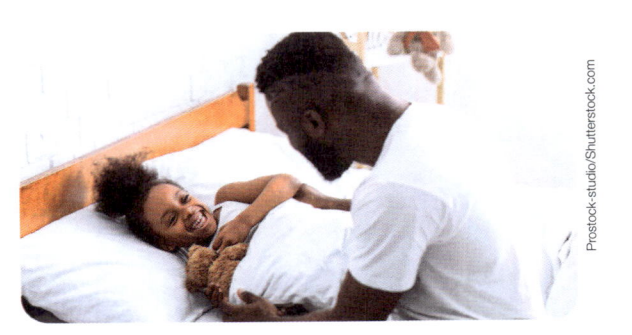

B)

2 BREAK THE CODES AND WRITE THE GREETINGS.

D	F	G	H	I	M	N	O	R	T
♥	🔑	🌼	👑	☀	⭐	🙂	🦋	➡	💬

A) GOOD MORNING

B) GOOD NIGHT

GOOD DEED

IT IS VERY IMPORTANT TO RESPECT YOUR FRIENDS!

I LEARNED THAT I LIKE MY FRIENDS AND RESPECT THEM.

LET'S PLAY

1 CAN YOU FIND US?

THE GOOD MORNING TRAIN IS COMING

THE GOOD MORNING **TRAIN** IS **COMING**,
HOW ARE YOU? CHOO-CHOO.
THE GOOD MORNING TRAIN IS COMING,
HOW ARE YOU? CHOO-CHOO.
GOOD MORNING, AMY.
HOW ARE YOU? CHOO-CHOO.
GOOD MORNING, BARRY.
HOW ARE YOU? CHOO-CHOO.
THE GOOD AFTERNOON TRAIN IS COMING,
HOW ARE YOU? CHOO-CHOO.
THE GOOD AFTERNOON TRAIN IS COMING,
HOW ARE YOU? CHOO-CHOO.
GOOD AFTERNOON, DAVID.
HOW ARE YOU? CHOO-CHOO.
GOOD AFTERNOON, RACHEL.
HOW ARE YOU? CHOO-CHOO.
THE GOOD EVENING TRAIN IS COMING,
HOW ARE YOU? CHOO-CHOO.
THE GOOD EVENING TRAIN IS COMING,
HOW ARE YOU? CHOO-CHOO.
GOOD EVENING, ETHAN.

LET'S SING!

HOW ARE YOU? CHOO-CHOO.
GOOD EVENING, MARIA.
HOW ARE YOU? CHOO-CHOO.
THE GOOD NIGHT TRAIN IS COMING,
HOW ARE YOU? CHOO-CHOO.
THE GOOD NIGHT TRAIN IS COMING,
HOW ARE YOU? CHOO-CHOO.
GOOD NIGHT, CHRISTIAN.
HOW ARE YOU? CHOO-CHOO.
GOOD NIGHT, KATE.
HOW ARE YOU? CHOO-CHOO.

POPULAR SONG. ADAPTED.

VOCABULARY

COMING (TO COME): VINDO (VIR).
HOW ARE YOU?: COMO VOCÊ ESTÁ/ VOCÊS ESTÃO?
TRAIN: TREM.

LET'S HAVE FUN

MOVIE TIME

WATCH A MOVIE WITH YOUR

F__IE__D__.

AFTER THIS UNIT I CAN

- RECOGNIZE BOOK CHARACTERS AND THEIR NAMES.
- SAY MY NAME.
- USE GREETINGS.
- IDENTIFY AND USE THE WORDS *BOY* AND *GIRL*.
- UNDERSTAND THE IMPORTANCE OF RESPECTING DIFFERENCES.

UNIT 2
I LOVE PETS

TODAY WE ARE GOING TO TALK ABOUT PETS.

THEY ARE CALLED DOMESTIC ANIMALS! WHO HAS A PET? THERE ARE DOGS, BIRDS, TURTLES, RABBITS, CATS, HAMSTERS, FISH, AND GUINEA PIGS!

VOCABULARY

BIRDS: PÁSSAROS.
DOMESTIC ANIMALS: ANIMAIS DOMÉSTICOS.
FISH: PEIXES.
GUINEA PIGS: PORQUINHOS-DA-ÍNDIA.
HAMSTERS: *HAMSTERS*.
PETS: ANIMAIS DE ESTIMAÇÃO.
RABBITS: COELHOS.
TURTLES: TARTARUGAS.

TWENTY-SEVEN 27

COMPREHENSION

1 WHAT IS THE THEME OF THIS UNIT? CHECK.

2 LOOK AT THE ANIMALS. PASTE ONLY THE STICKERS WITH PETS.

NOW, TRACE THE WORDS.

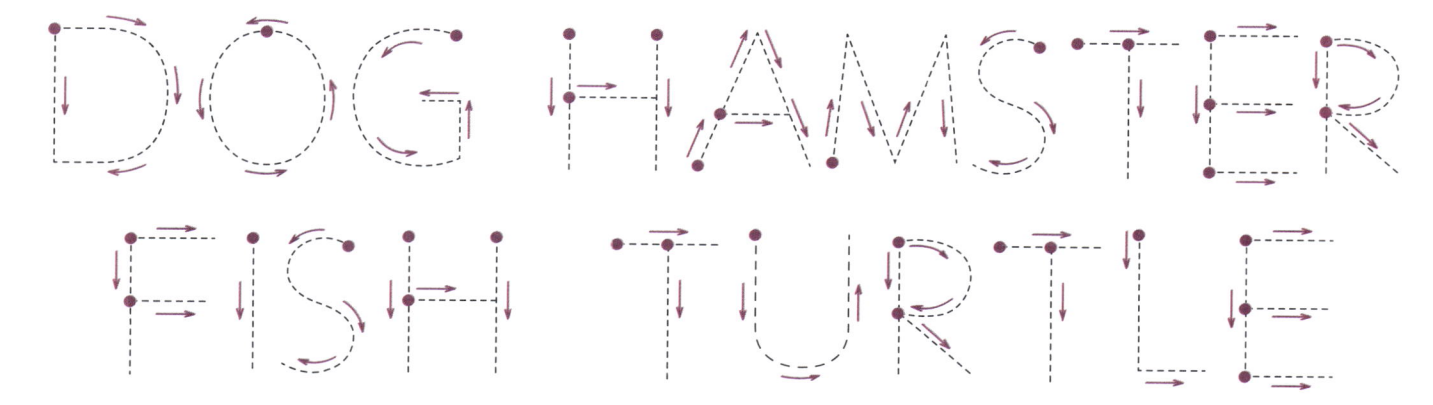

DOG HAMSTER
FISH TURTLE

LET'S PLAY

1 HELP EACH PET FIND ITS FOOD.

2 COLOR THE PETS.

A) ELEPHANT

B) GUINEA PIG

C) LION

D) DOG

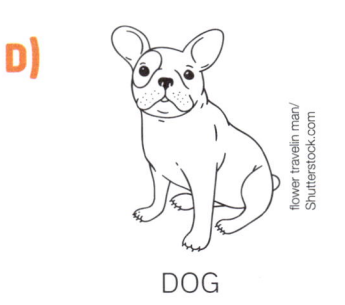

3 USE THE CODE BELOW TO COLOR THE ANIMALS. THEN WRITE THE NAMES.

🟡 HORSE　　🟢 HAMSTER　　🔵 RABBIT　　🟠 BIRD

_____　_____　_____　_____

4 WHOSE BIRTHDAY IS IT? WRITE.

GOOD DEED

TAKING CARE OF PETS
COLOR THE CORRECT ACTION.

DIGITAL PLAY

WHAT DO THEY EAT?
FIND OUT WHAT YOUR PET EATS.

LET'S SING!

FISH STORY

ONE, TWO, THREE, FOUR, FIVE?
ONCE I **CAUGHT** A FISH **ALIVE**.

SIX, SEVEN, EIGHT, NINE, TEN?
THEN I **LET IT GO AGAIN**.

ELEVEN, TWELVE, THIRTEEN, FOURTEEN, FIFTEEN?
IT COULD NOT **BE SEEN**.

WHY DID I LET IT GO?
BECAUSE IT **BIT** MY FINGER SO!

WHICH FINGER DID IT BITE?
THE **LITTLE FINGER** ON THE RIGHT!

NURSERY RHYME. ADAPTED.

VOCABULARY

AGAIN: NOVAMENTE.
ALIVE: VIVO(A).
BECAUSE: PORQUE.
BE SEEN: SER VISTO(A).
BIT (TO BITE): MORDEU (MORDER).
CAUGHT (TO CATCH): PEGUEI (PEGAR).
LET IT GO: DEIXEI IR (DEIXAR IR).
LITTLE FINGER: DEDO MINDINHO.
ONCE: UMA VEZ.

LET'S LISTEN

1 LISTEN AND COLOR THE CORRECT WORD.

THE LION IS   BIG.
                SMALL.

THE CAT IS.   BIG.
                SMALL.

THE ELEPHANT IS   BIG.
                    SMALL.

ENGLISH AROUND THE WORLD

WILD ANIMALS AROUND THE WORLD

LOOK AT PICTURES AND COLOR THE NAMES.

KANGAROO

BADGER

BEAVER

MOOSE

BALD EAGLE

GRIZZLY BEAR

LET'S PLAY

1 PASTE THE STICKERS OF THE WILD ANIMALS.

2 DIFFERENT AND FUNNY BREEDS OF DOGS AND CATS.

AFTER THIS UNIT I CAN

RECOGNIZE PETS AND WILD ANIMALS.

FIND OUT WHAT PETS EAT.

REVIEW THE COLORS IN ENGLISH.

USE THE ADJECTIVES *SMALL* AND *BIG* CORRECTLY.

THIRTY-FIVE 35

UNIT 3
A SPECIAL PLACE, THE SCHOOL!

> GOOD AFTERNOON! **MY NAME IS** JUDY. I AM YOUR **TEACHER**. **WHAT'S YOUR** NAME?

> MY NAME IS KATE! WHAT'S YOUR NAME?

> MY NAME IS ANNE. WHAT'S YOUR NAME?

> MY NAME IS JOHNNY. AND YOU? WHAT'S YOUR NAME?

> MY NAME IS TOM. WHAT'S YOUR NAME?

VOCABULARY

MY NAME IS: MEU NOME É.
TEACHER: PROFESSOR(A).
WHAT'S: QUAL É.
YOUR: SEU/SUA.

MY NAME IS _____

COMPREHENSION

1 WHO IS JUDY?
- ☐ A STUDENT.
- ☐ A TEACHER.

2 WHAT DOES THE TEACHER SAY?
- ☐ GOOD MORNING.
- ☐ GOOD AFTERNOON.

3 WHAT'S YOUR NAME?

A) MY NAME IS

B) MY NAME IS

C) MY NAME IS

D) MY NAME IS

LET'S PLAY

1 COMPLETE THE CROSSWORD PUZZLE.

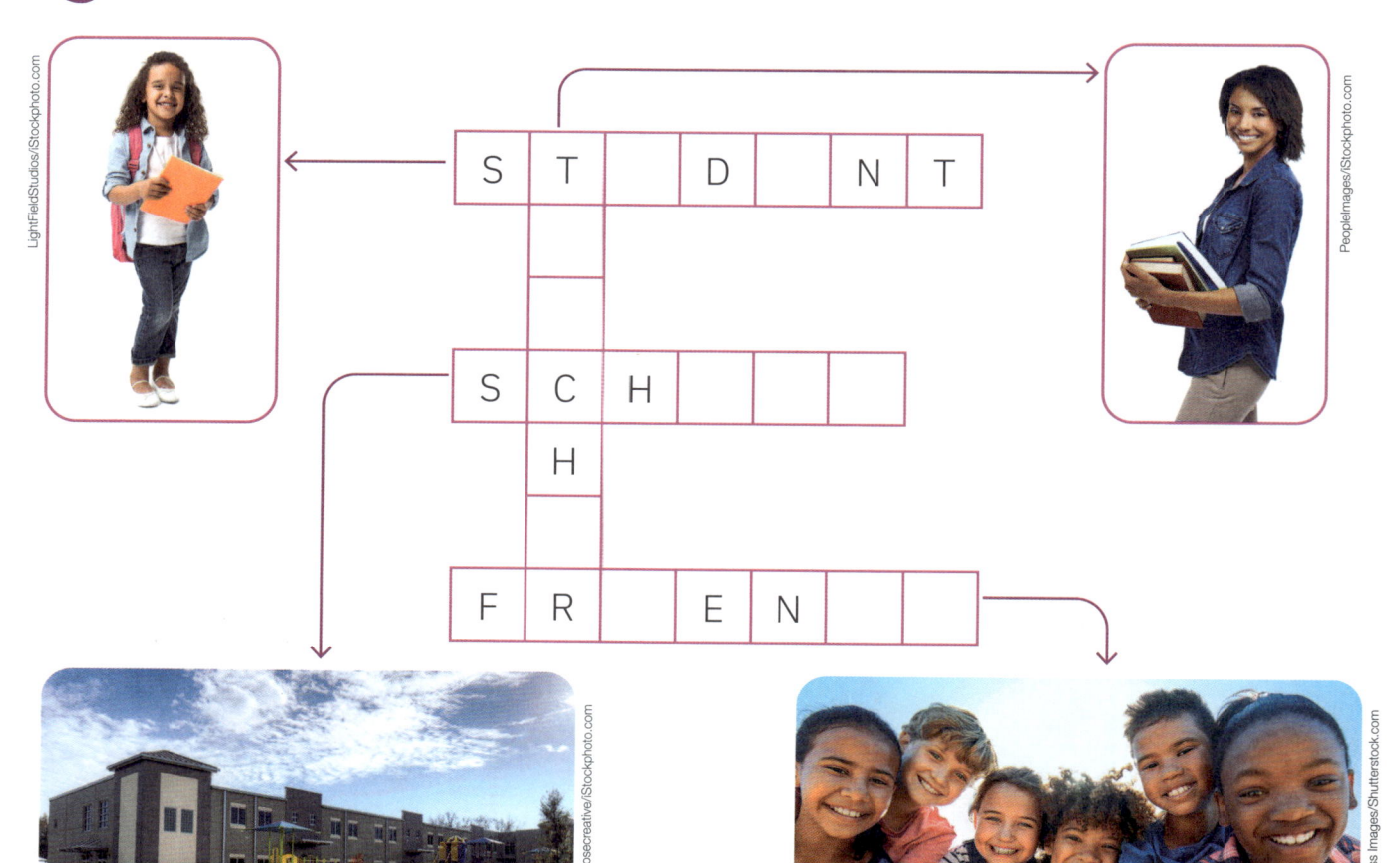

S T _ D _ N T

S C H _ _ _

H

F R _ E N _ _

DIGITAL PLAY

LET'S PLAY A QUIZ!

HOW MANY BOOKS DO YOU SEE IN THE PICTURE?
TRACE THE ANSWER: THREE

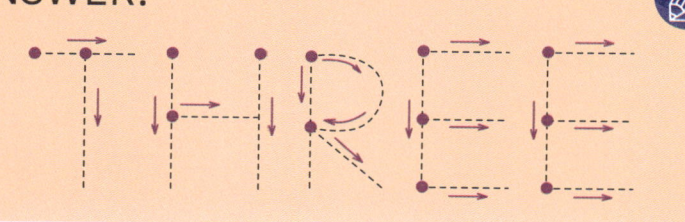

LET'S LISTEN

1 LISTEN, REPEAT, AND COLOR.

> PAY ATTENTION, STUDENTS! TODAY WE ARE GOING TO LEARN THE ALPHABET.

> A B C D E F G H I J K L M N O P Q R S T U V W X Y Z.

> ALL THE LETTERS AND LOTS OF WORDS!

> ALL THE LETTERS, TEACHER?

A B C D E F G H I
J K L M N O P Q R
S T U V W X Y Z

THIRTY-NINE **39**

LET'S PLAY

1 PASTE THE STICKERS AND WRITE.

ENGLISH AROUND THE WORLD

LOOK AND TELL THE DIFFERENCES.

A ESCOLA É UM LUGAR MUITO ESPECIAL. NELA, FAZEMOS AMIGOS E APRENDEMOS COISAS IMPORTANTES PARA O NOSSO FUTURO.

VOCÊ SABIA QUE NO MUNDO INTEIRO AS CRIANÇAS VÃO PARA A ESCOLA? MUITAS ESCOLAS SÃO PARECIDAS COM AS ESCOLAS DO BRASIL, E OUTRAS SÃO DIFERENTES. VEJA ALGUMAS ESCOLAS EM OUTROS PAÍSES.

ALUNOS EM SALA DE AULA NA CHINA.

ALUNOS EM SALA DE AULA NA ÍNDIA.

ALUNOS UTILIZANDO *TABLET* EM UMA ESCOLA DE SINGAPURA.

ALUNOS DE UMA ESCOLA NOS EMIRADOS ÁRABES UNIDOS.

LET'S PLAY

1 READ AND TRACE THE LETTERS.

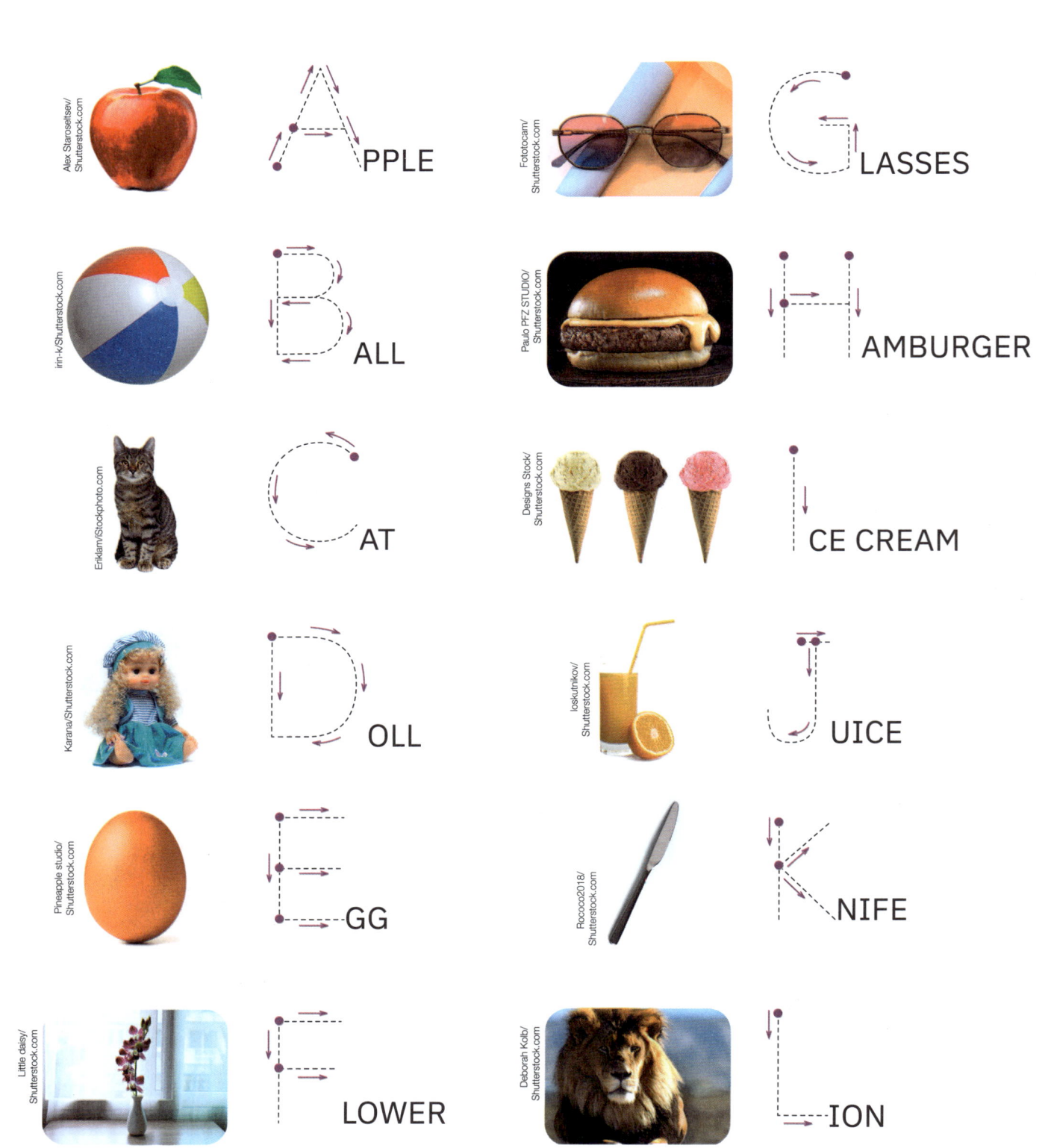

Apple

Ball

Cat

Doll

Egg

Flower

Glasses

Hamburger

Ice cream

Juice

Knife

Lion

Milk

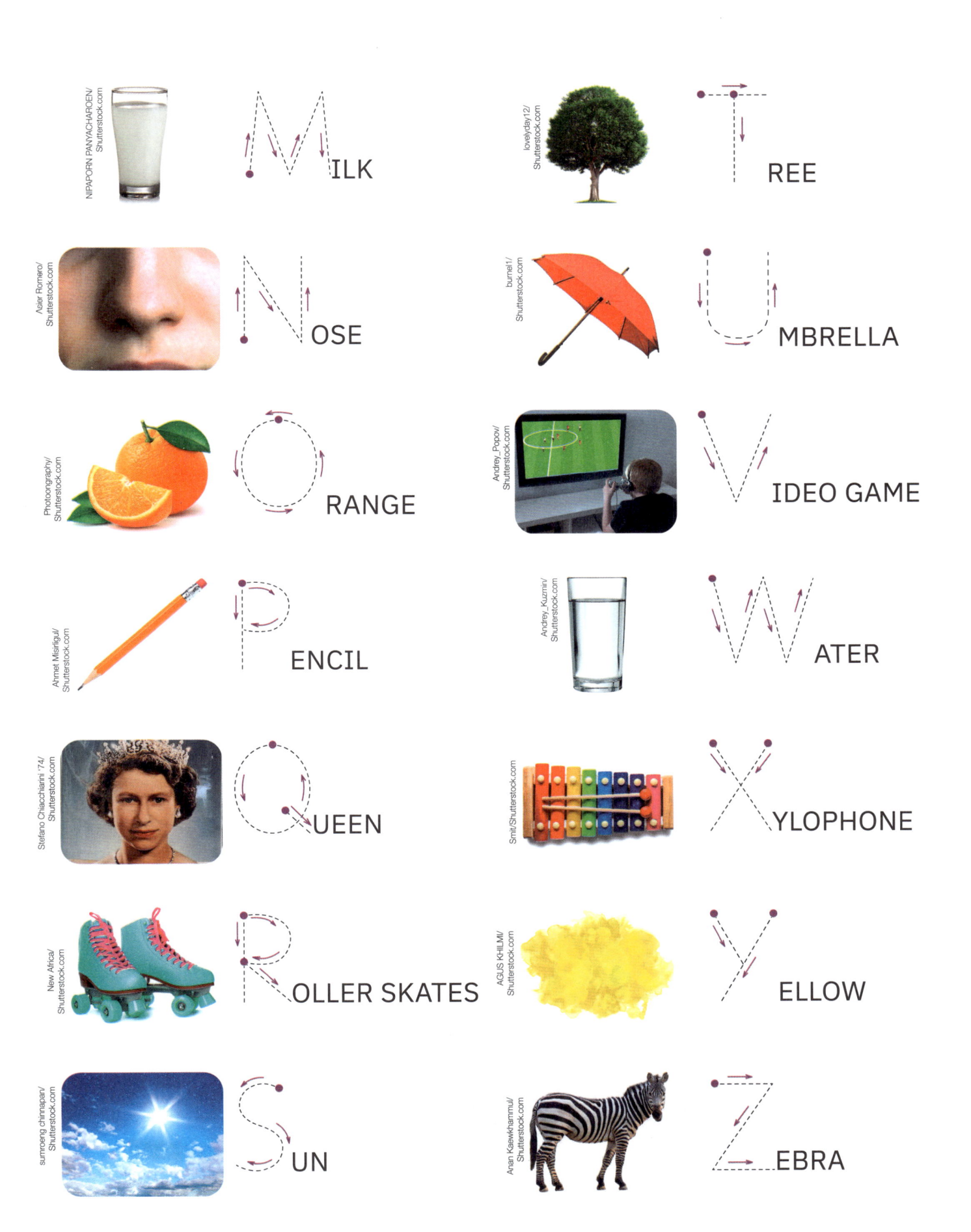

Nose

Orange

Pencil

Queen

Roller Skates

Sun

Tree

Umbrella

Video Game

Water

Xylophone

Yellow

Zebra

HELLO, HELLO, HELLO

HELLO, HELLO, HELLO.
MY **NAME** IS AMY.

HELLO, HELLO, HELLO.
MY NAME IS CHRISTIAN.

HELLO, HELLO, HELLO.
MY NAME IS RACHEL.

HELLO, HELLO, HELLO.
MY NAME IS ETHAN.

HELLO, HELLO, HELLO.
WHAT IS YOUR NAME?

HELLO, HELLO, HELLO.
MY NAME IS _____.

SPECIALLY WRITTEN FOR THIS BOOK.

LET'S SING!

VOCABULARY

NAME: NOME.
WHAT: O QUE/QUAL.

LET'S PLAY

1 COUNT AND WRITE.

A) HOW MANY BOYS?

B) HOW MANY GIRLS?

VOCABULARY

HOW MANY: QUANTOS/QUANTAS.

- **1:** ONE.
- **2:** TWO.
- **3:** THREE.
- **4:** FOUR.
- **5:** FIVE.
- **6:** SIX.
- **7:** SEVEN.
- **8:** EIGHT.
- **9:** NINE.
- **10:** TEN.
- **11:** ELEVEN.
- **12:** TWELVE.
- **13:** THIRTEEN.
- **14:** FOURTEEN.
- **15:** FIFTEEN.
- **16:** SIXTEEN.
- **17:** SEVENTEEN.
- **18:** EIGHTEEN.
- **19:** NINETEEN.
- **20:** TWENTY.

LET'S LISTEN

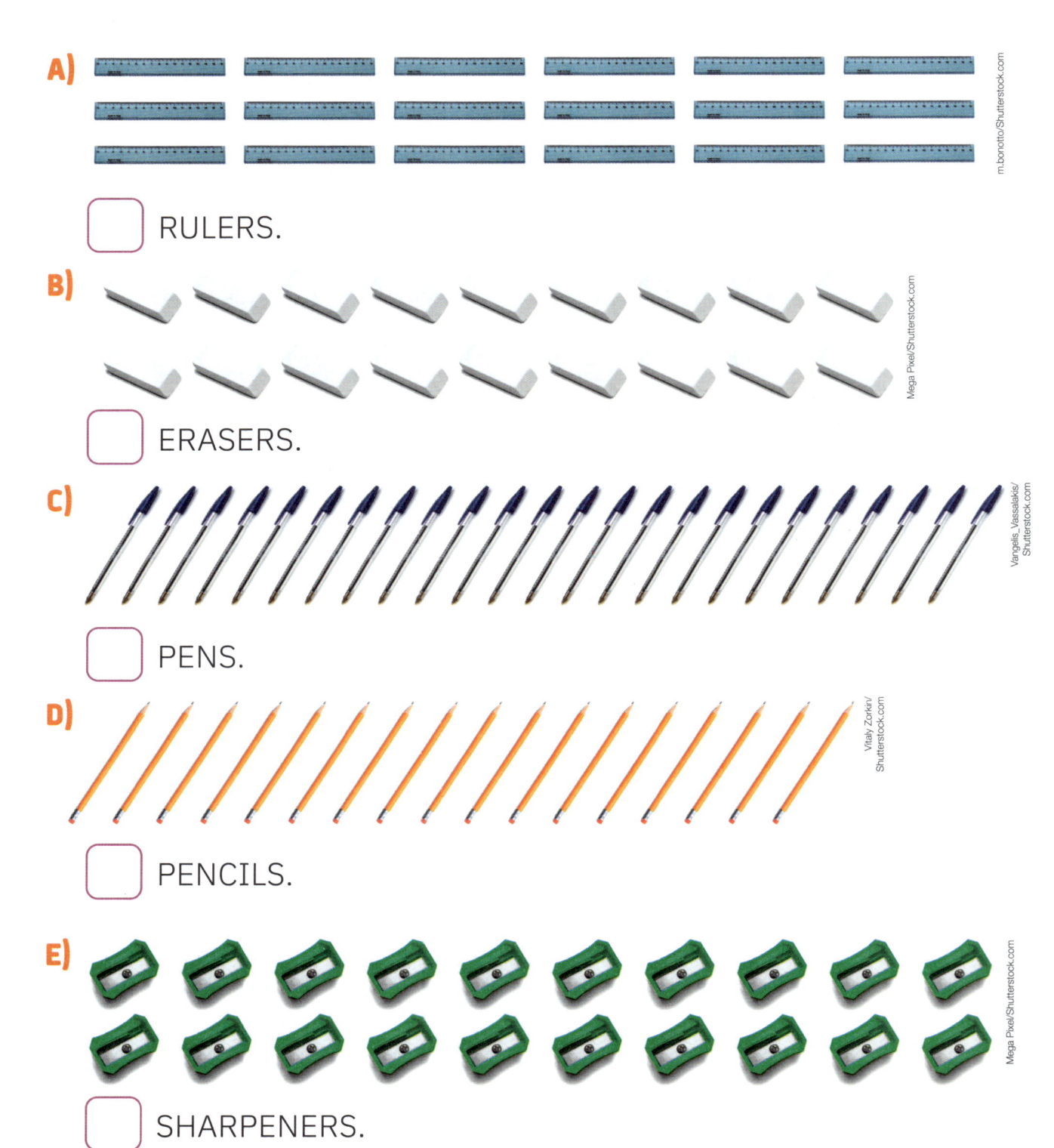

1 HOW MANY? LISTEN, CIRCLE, AND WRITE.

A) ☐ RULERS.

B) ☐ ERASERS.

C) ☐ PENS.

D) ☐ PENCILS.

E) ☐ SHARPENERS.

GOOD DEED

GREETINGS & MANNERS

CREATE A POSTER TO STIMULATE GOOD MANNERS.

Thank you! Good job! Good night!
I'm sorry!
Good morning! Good evening!
Good afternoon! Please.

AFTER THIS UNIT I CAN

	😊	😐	☹
ASK PEOPLE'S NAMES.			
NAME SOME SCHOOL OBJECTS.			
IDENTIFY THE LETTERS OF THE ALPHABET IN ENGLISH.			
COUNT FROM 1 TO 20 IN ENGLISH.			
UNDERSTAND THE DIFFERENCES AND SIMILARITIES AMONG SCHOOLS AROUND THE WORLD.			

UNIT 4
MY FAVORITE FOOD

MY FAVORITE FOOD IS ICE CREAM, BUT TODAY I AM HAVING A **PIECE OF CAKE**. WHAT IS YOUR FAVORITE FOOD, GUYS?

MY FAVORITE FOOD IS **RICE**, **BEANS**, AND **MEAT**, BUT TODAY I AM HAVING A **FRUIT SALAD**.

MY FAVORITE FOOD IS **PASTA**, BUT TODAY I AM HAVING A **SANDWICH**.

VOCABULARY

BEANS: FEIJÃO.
FRUIT SALAD: SALADA DE FRUTAS.
ICE CREAM: SORVETE.
MEAT: CARNE.
MY FAVORITE FOOD IS: MINHA COMIDA FAVORITA É.
PASTA: MACARRÃO.
PIECE OF CAKE: PEDAÇO DE BOLO.
RICE: ARROZ.
SANDWICH: SANDUÍCHE.

COMPREHENSION

1 WHAT ARE THE BOYS TALKING ABOUT? CHECK.

☐ TOYS　　　☐ FOOD　　　☐ PETS

2 PASTE THE STICKER AND WRITE.

_____

3 WHO LIKES ICE CREAM?

☐ TOM　　　☐ JOHNNY　　　☐ TERRY

LET'S LISTEN

1 LISTEN, REPEAT, AND CIRCLE.

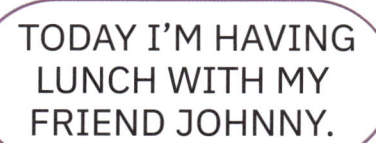

- TODAY I'M HAVING LUNCH WITH MY FRIEND JOHNNY.
- WE'RE HAVING HAMBURGER, JUICE, AND CAKE.

GOOD DEED

FOOD DONATION CAMPAIGN!

SHARE WITH LOVE!

THE HEALTHY FOODS ARE...

- ☐ VEGETABLES, GREENS, AND FRUIT.
- ☐ SWEETS, FRIED FOODS, FATS.

LET'S PLAY

1 JOHNNY WANTS TO HAVE BREAKFAST. HELP HIM.

GRAMMAR POINT

SUBJECT PRONOUNS

I

I LIKE APPLES.

YOU

YOU LIKE PEACHES.

LET'S PLAY

1 COMPLETE. USE **I** OR **YOU**.

A) _____ LIKE ICE CREAM.

B) _____ LIKE TO EAT BREAD AND BUTTER.

C) _____ EAT CARROTS AND BEETS.

D) _____ LOVE PASTA.

LET'S LISTEN

1 LISTEN, ANSWER, AND COLOR.

○ WHITE ● RED ● GREEN

A) WHAT COLOR IS THE RICE?

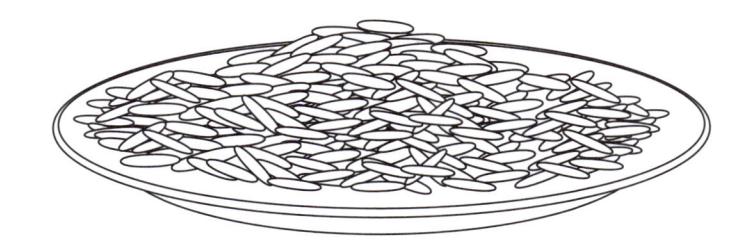

THE RICE IS _____.

B) WHAT COLOR IS THE SALAD?

THE SALAD IS _____.

C) WHAT COLOR IS THE MEAT?

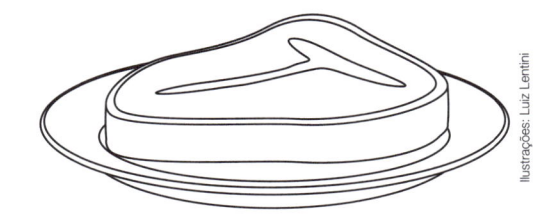

THE MEAT IS _____.

DIGITAL PLAY

MY FUN FOOD

WOW! DELICIOUS!

HEALTHY FOOD IS FUN!

LET'S PLAY

1 FIND THE FOOD ITEMS IN THE WORDSEARCH.

A) BEANS **B)** PASTA **C)** MEAT **D)** RICE

F	I	S	H	A	I	U	N	S	A	L	A	D	B
A	B	E	A	N	S	O	M	H	U	J	Ç	Z	V
X	T	G	H	D	K	L	P	A	S	T	A	M	D
M	E	A	T	G	T	E	W	A	V	C	N	K	L
D	L	N	V	F	R	U	I	T	S	P	K	I	R
R	O	C	R	I	C	E	D	E	Q	A	L	K	N
J	U	I	L	E	O	P	C	H	I	C	K	E	N

E) SALAD **F)** FISH **G)** CHICKEN **H)** FRUIT

FIVE FAT SAUSAGES

FIVE **FAT SAUSAGES**
SIZZLING IN A **PAN**.
ONE **WENT** POP,
THE **OTHER** WENT BANG!
FOUR FAT SAUSAGES
SIZZLING IN A PAN.
ONE WENT POP,
THE OTHER WENT BANG!
THREE FAT SAUSAGES
SIZZLING IN A PAN.
ONE WENT POP,
THE OTHER WENT BANG!
TWO FAT SAUSAGES
SIZZLING IN A PAN.
ONE WENT POP,
THE OTHER WENT BANG!
ONE FAT SAUSAGE
SIZZLING IN A PAN.
ONE WENT POP,
THE OTHER WENT BANG!
NO FAT SAUSAGES SIZZLING IN A PAN!

NURSERY RHYME.

LET'S SING!

VOCABULARY

FAT: GORDO(A).
OTHER: OUTRO(A).
PAN: PANELA.
SAUSAGE: SALSICHA.
SIZZLING (TO SIZZLE): CHIANDO (CHIAR).
WENT (TO GO): FOI (IR).

LET'S PLAY

1 TIME TO EAT! WRITE YOUR FAVORITE BREAKFAST FOOD.

_____
_____
_____
_____

2 TRACE THE WORD BELOW.

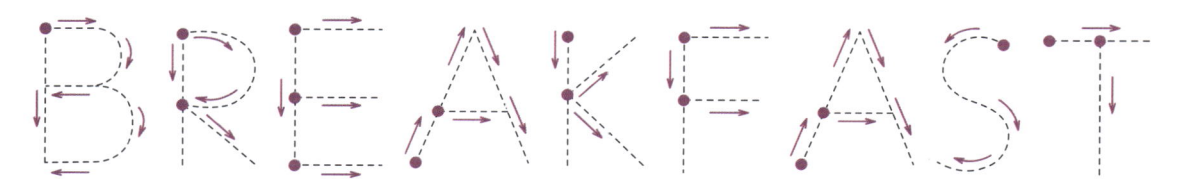

BREAKFAST

ENGLISH AROUND THE WORLD

DIFFERENT BREAKFAST

IDENTIFY THE CORRECT BREAKFAST AND PASTE THE STICKERS.

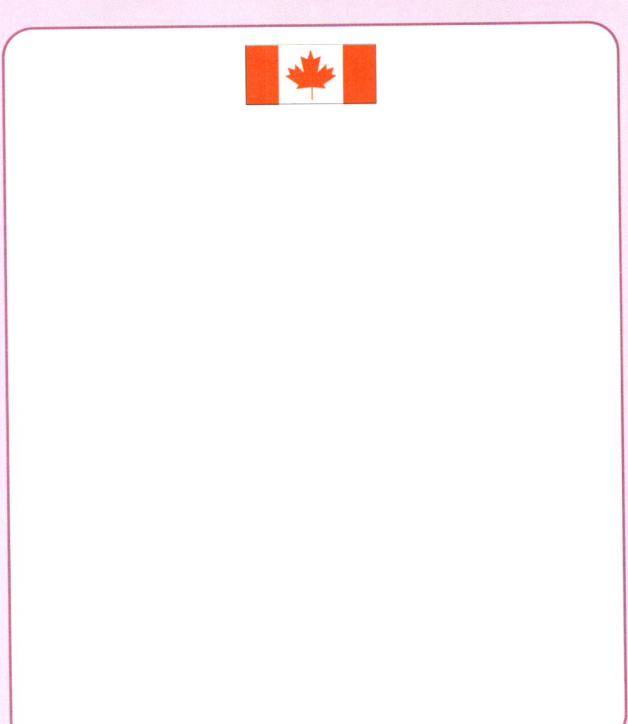

AFTER THIS UNIT I CAN

- RECOGNIZE HEALTHY FOODS.
- IDENTIFY THE NAMES AND COLORS OF DIFFERENT FOODS.
- REFLECT ON THE IMPORTANCE OF A BALANCED DIET.
- UNDERSTAND THE DIFFERENT TYPES OF BREAKFAST IN COUNTRIES LIKE THE UNITED STATES AND CANADA.
- TALK ABOUT FAVORITE FOODS.

UNIT 5
SUMMER VACATION

> I LOVE THE **BEACH**. I'M VERY HAPPY! LOOK AT THE **SEA**, THE **SAND**, THE SUN, AND THE **SKY**! I CAN PLAY WITH MY BEACH **TOYS**.

VOCABULARY

BEACH: PRAIA.
BUCKET: BALDE.
PARASOL: GUARDA-SOL.
SAND: AREIA.

SEA: MAR.
SHOVEL: PÁ.
SKY: CÉU.
TOYS: BRINQUEDOS.

COMPREHENSION

1 TERRY TALKS ABOUT...

☐ ANIMALS.

☐ BEACH TOYS.

2 WRITE YOUR FAVORITE TOY.

MY FAVORITE TOY IS...

3 FIND AND CIRCLE SIX DIFFERENCES.

LET'S PLAY

1 MATCH PICTURES AND WORDS.

BOAT

HORSE

BEACH TOYS

CAMPSITE

2 READ, TRACE, AND COLOR.

USE **BROWN** AND **RED** TO COLOR THE BOAT, **BLUE** TO COLOR THE SKY, **GREEN** TO COLOR THE SEA, AND **YELLOW** TO COLOR THE SUN.

BLUE

RED

GREEN

YELLOW

BROWN

3 COMPLETE THE CROSSWORD.

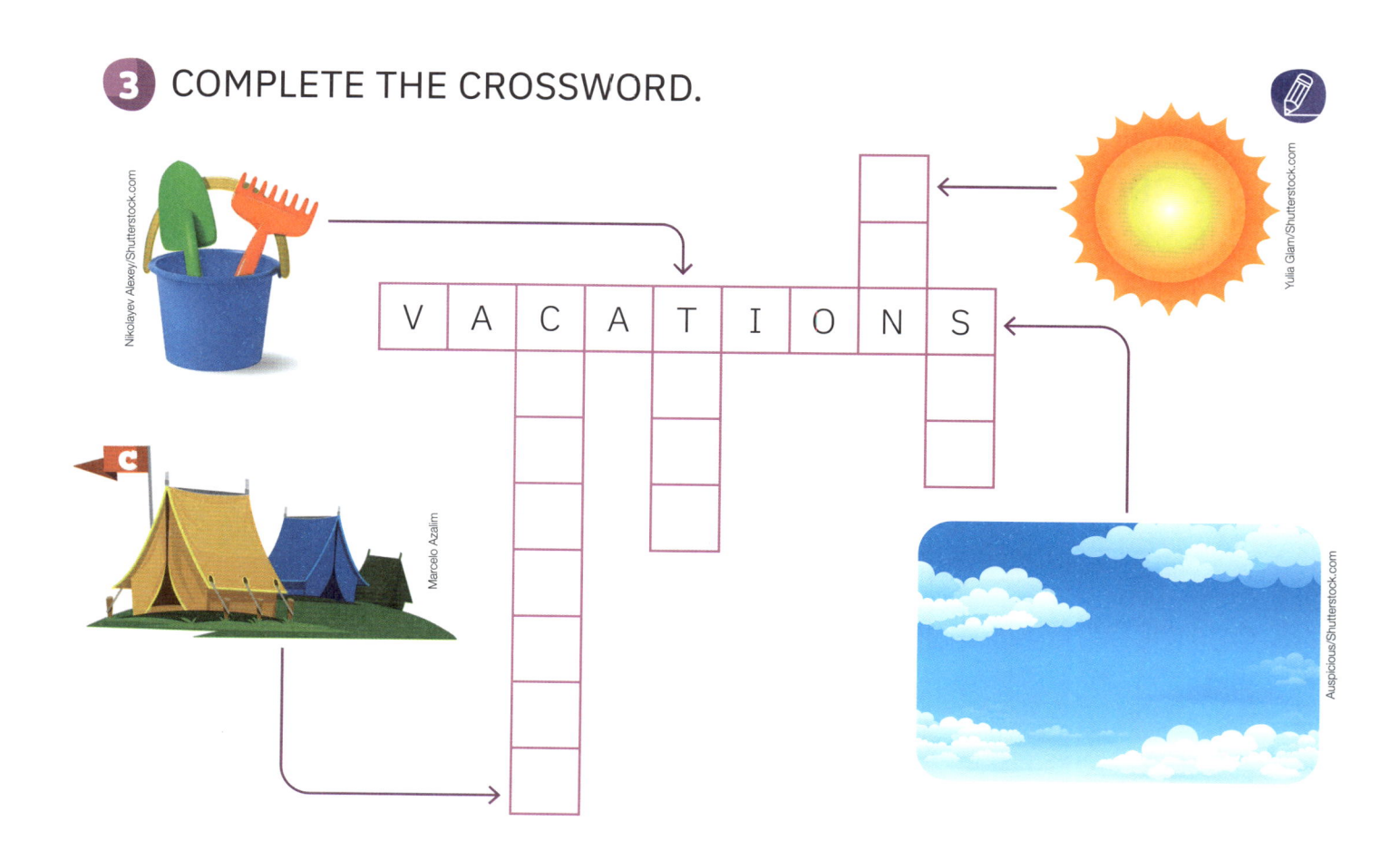

V A C A T I O N S

GRAMMAR POINT

SUBJECT PRONOUNS

WE ⟶ NÓS

ANNE AND I ARE ON VACATION.
WE ARE ON VACATION.

THEY ⟶ ELES/ELAS

KATE, DAVID, AND TOM ARE ON VACATION.
THEY ARE ON VACATION.

LET'S PLAY

1 READ AND CHOOSE.

A) **MEGAN AND I** ARE GOING TO THE BEACH.

☐ WE ☐ THEY

B) **GARY AND CLAUDIA** ARE IN THE CAMPSITE.

☐ WE ☐ THEY

2 COMPLETE THE SENTENCES WITH **WE** OR **THEY**.

A) ANNE, TERRY, AND I LIKE TO PLAY WITH TOYS.

_____ LIKE TO PLAY WITH TOYS.

B) JOHNNY AND TOM ARE GOOD FRIENDS.

_____ ARE GOOD FRIENDS.

GOOD DEED

TAKE CARE OF NATURE

LET'S MAKE A CAMPAIGN TO CLEAN NATURE!

A SAILOR WENT TO SEA, SEA, SEA

LET'S SING!

A **SAILOR WENT** TO **SEA**, SEA, SEA,
TO SEE WHAT HE COULD **SEE**, SEE, SEE.
BUT ALL HE COULD SEE, SEE, SEE
WAS THE **BOTTOM** OF
THE **DEEP** BLUE SEA, SEA, SEA.
A SAILOR WENT TO SEA, SEA, SEA,
TO SEE WHAT HE COULD SEE, SEE, SEE.
BUT ALL HE COULD SEE, SEE, SEE
WAS THE BOTTOM OF
THE DEEP BLUE SEA, SEA, SEA.

TRADITIONAL RHYME.

VOCABULARY

BOTTOM: FUNDO.
DEEP: PROFUNDO.
SAILOR: MARINHEIRO(A).
SEA: MAR.
SEE (TO SEE): VER.
WENT (TO GO): FOI (IR).

LET'S PLAY

1 NUMBER THE TOYS.

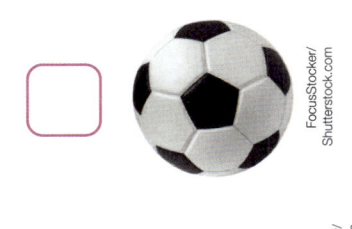

1. BALL
2. DOLL
3. BUCKET
4. SHOVEL

2 DRAW YOUR FRIEND AND HIS/HER FAVORITE TOY.

3 FIND THE OBJECTS IN THE WORDSEARCH.

TOYS  BOAT  BALL

T	O	Y	S	E	T	V	S	O	W	T	O	K
S	D	F	H	P	A	R	A	S	O	L	D	K
C	R	E	F	F	G	G	E	R	W	T	K	R
U	D	S	H	O	V	E	L	S	E	O	P	A
H	E	F	B	N	G	R	T	H	M	K	Y	U
B	S	S	H	B	U	C	K	E	T	Q	I	O
O	S	I	N	K	M	L	P	S	T	G	V	E
F	C	N	G	B	V	D	B	O	A	T	G	H
R	Y	L	E	B	I	Y	M	F	W	E	S	H
S	L	I	N	B	A	L	L	H	X	S	K	L

BUCKET  SHOVEL  PARASOL

DIGITAL PLAY

MY FAVORITE KIND OF TRIP!

MY FAVORITE KIND OF TRIP IS…

LET'S PLAY

1 HELP THE FATHER AND SON GET TO THE CAMPSITE.

SIXTY-SEVEN

LET'S LISTEN

1 WHERE DO YOU WANT TO SPEND YOUR SUMMER VACATION?

VOCABULARY

BEACH: PRAIA.
COUNTRYSIDE: INTERIOR.
SPEND: PASSAR.
VACATION: FÉRIAS.
WANT (TO WANT): QUER/QUERER.
WHERE: ONDE.

ENGLISH AROUND THE WORLD

DIFFERENT KINDS OF TRIPS FOR KIDS

WHAT WAS YOUR FAVORITE TRIP?

AFTER THIS UNIT I CAN

IDENTIFY DIFFERENT PLACES AND LEISURE ACTIVITIES.
USE THE PERSONAL PRONOUNS *WE* AND *THEY* CORRECTLY.
REVIEW THE COLORS.

68 SIXTY-EIGHT

UNIT 6
OUR FAMILY

LOOK, THIS IS MY FAMILY! MY **FATHER** JOHN, MY **GRANDFATHER** VINCENT, MY **UNCLE** TOM, MY **AUNT** BETTY, MY **COUSIN** THEO, MY **BROTHER** KEVIN, MY **MOTHER** LOUISE, MY **SISTER** SILVIA, AND MY **GRANDMOTHER** OLIVIA.

WOW! WHAT A GREAT FAMILY!!

📖 VOCABULARY

AUNT: TIA.
BROTHER: IRMÃO.
COUSIN: PRIMO/PRIMA.
FATHER: PAI.
GRANDFATHER: AVÔ.
GRANDMOTHER: AVÓ.
MOTHER: MÃE.
SISTER: IRMÃ.
UNCLE: TIO.

COMPREHENSION

1 WHAT ARE YOU STUDYING?

☐ NUMBERS.

☐ FAMILY MEMBERS.

2 WHO IS VINCENT?

☐ MEGAN'S FATHER.

☐ MEGAN'S GRANDFATHER.

3 DO YOU HAVE A SISTER OR A BROTHER? WHAT ARE THEIR NAMES?

_____

_____

_____

4 WHO ARE THEY? LOOK AND WRITE.

A) _____

C) _____

B) _____

D) _____

NOW, COMPLETE THE CROSSWORD.

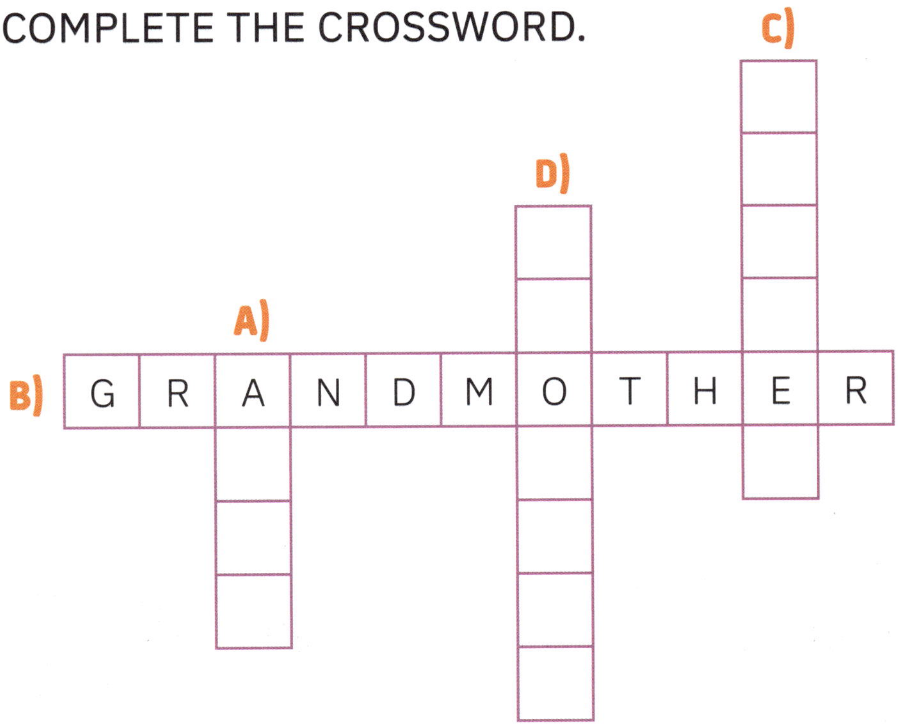

B) G R A N D M O T H E R

5 TRACE THE WORD.

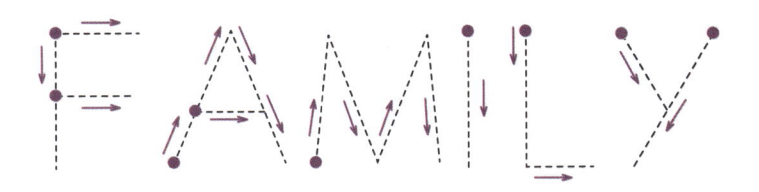

FAMILY

LET'S LISTEN

1 LISTEN AND REPEAT. THEN COLOR THE CHILDREN.

GRAMMAR POINT

SUBJECT PRONOUNS

SHE

MARY IS KATE'S MOM.

SHE IS KATE'S MOM.

HE

SCOTT IS KATE'S DAD.

HE IS KATE'S DAD.

2 LISTEN AND PASTE THE STICKERS IN THE CORRECT COLUMN.

SHE	HE

ENGLISH AROUND THE WORLD

OTHER WORDS FOR MOTHER AND FATHER

MOTHER (INFORMAL)	
BRITISH	AMERICAN
MUM MUMMY	MOM MOMMY MA MAM

FATHER (INFORMAL)	
BRITISH	AMERICAN
DAD DADDY POPS	DAD DADDY PA

LET'S PLAY

1 LOOK AT MEGAN'S FAMILY PHOTO. WRITE **HE** OR **SHE** FOR EACH FAMILY MEMBER.

BETTY   LOUISE   VINCENT   JOHN   TOM

THEO   SILVIA   KEVIN   MEGAN   OLIVIA

A) JOHN
_____

B) VINCENT
_____

C) SILVIA
_____

D) BETTY
_____

E) THEO
_____

F) KEVIN
_____

G) LOUISE
_____

H) TOM
_____

I) OLIVIA
_____

J) MEGAN
_____

DIGITAL PLAY

THESE ARE OUR FAMILIES!

TAKE A PHOTO OF YOUR FAMILY!

LET'S PLAY

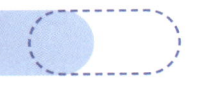

1 LOOK AND WRITE. HOW MANY PEOPLE ARE THERE?

LET'S SING!

THE FAMILY

MY FATHER IS A **BIG** MAN.
MY MOTHER IS A **WONDERFUL** WOMAN.
MY BROTHER IS A GOOD BOY.
MY SISTER IS A **PRETTY** GIRL.
AND I?
AND I?
I AM A **HAPPY KID**,
I **BELONG** TO A FAMILY
AND WE **LIVE TOGETHER**
WITH **LOVE**.

WRITTEN ESPECIALLY FOR THIS BOOK.

VOCABULARY

BELONG (TO BELONG): PERTENÇO (PERTENCER).
BIG: GRANDE.
HAPPY: FELIZ.
KID: CRIANÇA.
LIVE (TO LIVE): MORAMOS (MORAR).
LOVE: AMOR.
PRETTY: BONITO(A).
TOGETHER: JUNTOS(AS).
WONDERFUL: MARAVILHOSO(A).

GOOD DEED

WE MUST RESPECT EVERYONE

PEOPLE CAN PLAY DIFFERENT ROLES IN A FAMILY.

DRAW YOUR FAMILY AND NAME EACH MEMBER.

A) FAMILY MEMBERS WHO LIVE WITH YOU.

B) FAMILY MEMBERS WHO DON'T LIVE WITH YOU, BUT HELP AROUND THE HOUSE.

LET'S PLAY

1 MATCH AND COMPLETE.

A)

_____ IS A BOY.

B)

_____ IS A GIRL.

C)

_____ IS A MAN.

D)

_____ IS A WOMAN.

HE

SHE

2 LOOK AT THE PICTURES.

A)

B)

C)

D)

NOW, COUNT AND ANSWER.

A) HOW MANY FAMILIES ARE THERE?
_____

B) HOW MANY DAUGHTERS ARE THERE?
_____

C) HOW MANY SONS ARE THERE?
_____

D) HOW MANY ADULTS ARE THERE?
_____

E) IN HOW MANY FAMILIES IS THERE A MOTHER?
_____

F) IN HOW MANY FAMILIES ARE THERE GRANDPARENTS?
_____

SEVENTY-NINE

3 FIND AND CIRCLE THE WORDS.

**FATHER * MOTHER * SON * DAUGHTER * COUSIN
GRANDFATHER * GRANDMOTHER * UNCLE * AUNT**

T	F	A	T	H	E	R	J	T	R	J	K	L	V	C
B	B	H	J	K	D	R	P	Ç	D	V	T	R	U	R
G	T	M	R	G	R	A	N	D	F	A	T	H	E	R
U	N	C	L	E	Y	I	L	M	B	C	V	W	S	D
F	R	H	J	K	D	R	P	Ç	M	O	T	H	E	R
G	R	A	N	D	M	O	T	H	E	R	H	B	N	L
R	J	L	B	T	G	D	K	J	L	P	L	C	D	R
N	J	L	B	C	O	U	S	I	N	P	L	C	D	R
S	O	N	N	B	V	D	G	F	Z	B	A	U	N	T
N	D	E	W	R	T	D	A	U	G	H	T	E	R	Ç

AFTER THIS UNIT I CAN

ASK PEOPLE'S NAMES.
SAY THE NAMES OF FAMILY MEMBERS.
RECOGNIZE THE USE OF THE SUBJECT PRONOUNS *HE* AND *SHE*.
RECOGNIZE THE USE OF THE DEMONSTRATIVE PRONOUN *THIS*.
UNDERSTAND THAT THERE ARE DIFFERENT FAMILIES AND EACH OF THEIR MEMBERS PERFORMS DIFFERENT ROLES.

UNIT 7
HOME SWEET HOME

HELLO, MEGAN!

HI, TOM AND LUCY! **HOW ARE YOU?**

COME ON IN. WELCOME TO MY **HOME**!

YOUR HOUSE IS SO **CUTE**, LOUISE!

THANK YOU!

📖 VOCABULARY

COME ON IN (TO COME ON IN): ENTRE (ENTRAR).
CUTE: ADORÁVEL.
HELLO: OLÁ.
HI: OI.
HOME: CASA, LAR.
HOW ARE YOU? COMO VOCÊS ESTÃO?
THANK YOU: OBRIGADO(A).

EIGHTY-ONE

COMPREHENSION

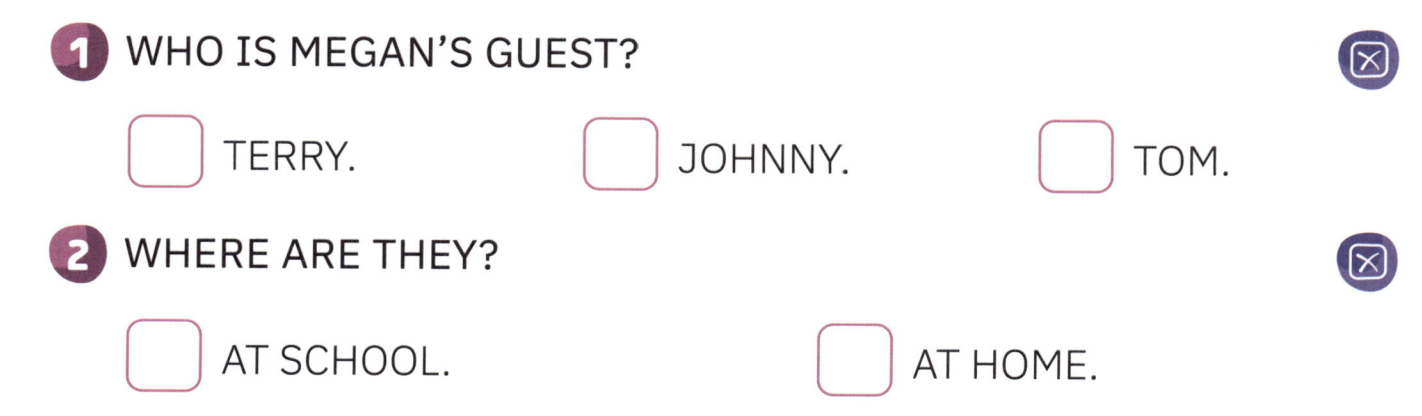

1 WHO IS MEGAN'S GUEST?

☐ TERRY.   ☐ JOHNNY.   ☐ TOM.

2 WHERE ARE THEY?

☐ AT SCHOOL.   ☐ AT HOME.

3 DRAW THE SCENE.

LET'S PLAY

1 COLOR THE PATH AND HELP TOM FIND HIS HOME.

2 LOOK AND WRITE.

1. BEDROOM (QUARTO)

2.

3.

4. KITCHEN (COZINHA)

3 IDENTIFY THE SHAPES AND MATCH.

A) ROOF

B) DOOR

C) WINDOW

SQUARE

TRIANGLE

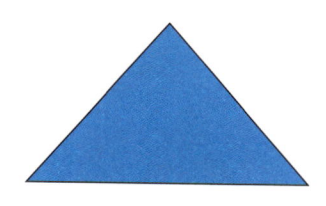

RECTANGLE

LET'S LISTEN

1 WHAT'S IN THE KITCHEN? LISTEN AND NUMBER THE OBJECTS.

2 WHAT'S IN THE LIVING ROOM? LISTEN AND PASTE THE STICKERS.

LET'S PLAY

1 DRAW A LINE THROUGH THE IMAGES RELATING TO THE HOUSE.

GRAMMAR POINT

INTERROGATIVE PRONOUNS

WHO → QUEM (PESSOAS)

WHO IS THAT BOY?

HE IS JOHNNY.

WHERE → ONDE (LUGARES)

WHERE IS THE SKIRT?

IT IS IN MY BEDROOM.

LET'S PLAY

1 FIND OUT THE MISSING OBJECTS. LOOK, READ, AND WRITE.

THIS IS MY ROOM.

WARDROBE — SHELF — DESK — BEDSIDE TABLE — BED — LAMP — MIRROR — RUG

WHAT'S MISSING?

_____
_____

2 READ AND COLOR.

SHOWER

MOM, I NEED SHAMPOO, SOAP, AND A TOWEL.

TOILET SEAT

BATHTUB

SINK

LET'S SING!

THAT IS MY HOUSE

LOOK AT THAT HOUSE
ON THAT **STREET**.
I LIVE IN THAT HOUSE,
THAT'S MY HOUSE.
LOOK AT THE ROOF
ON THAT HOUSE,
ON THAT STREET.
I LIVE IN THAT HOUSE,
THAT'S MY HOUSE.
LOOK AT THAT **CHIMNEY**,
ON THAT **ROOF**,
ON THAT HOUSE,
ON THAT STREET.
I LIVE IN THAT HOUSE,
THAT'S MY HOUSE.
LOOK AT THAT CAT
ON THAT CHIMNEY,
ON THAT ROOF,
ON THAT HOUSE,
ON THAT STREET.
I LIVE IN THAT
I LIVE IN THAT HOUSE,
THAT'S MY HOUSE.

CUMULATIVE SONG.

VOCABULARY

CHIMNEY: CHAMINÉ.
LOOK (TO LOOK): VEJA (VER).
ROOF: TELHADO.
STREET: RUA.

ENGLISH AROUND THE WORLD

FIND OUT DIFFERENT TYPES OF HOUSES AROUND THE WORLD.

DIGITAL PLAY

MY ROOM!

TAKE A PICTURE OF YOUR ROOM.

GOOD DEED

WE MUST RESPECT OUR NEIGHBORS

PROMOTE A GOOD DEED BY TAKING A SOUVENIR OR HELPING ONE OF YOUR NEIGHBORS.

LET'S PLAY

1 FIND WAYS FOR THE RESIDENTS TO COME TO THE NEW NEIGHBOR'S HOUSE AND CELEBRATE.

LET'S HAVE FUN

1 A WELCOME PARTY! WRITE THE INVITATION.

Welcome to our PARTY!

HELLO! PLEASE VISIT OUR CLASSROOM.

WE WILL BE HAPPY!

DATE: _____

TIME: _____

PLACE: _____

AFTER THIS UNIT I CAN

- LEARN AND USE THE NAME OF THE ROOMS AND OBJECTS IN THE HOUSE.
- REFLECT ON THE IMPORTANCE OF A SAFE HOME.
- KNOW THE DIFFERENT TYPES OF HOUSES, ESPECIALLY IN THE USA AND CANADA.
- RECOGNIZE GEOMETRIC SHAPES AND EXPAND VOCABULARY IN ENGLISH.

UNIT 8
MY CLOTHES

WHAT SHOULD I WEAR ON DAVID'S BIRTHDAY? LET'S SEE! A **DRESS**, A **SHIRT**, A **T-SHIRT**, A **COAT**, **PANTS**, **A PAIR OF BOOTS**, OR A PAIR OF SHOES?

IN MY OPINION, YOU SHOULD WEAR A DRESS AND A PAIR OF **SHOES**. DO NOT FORGET THE **SOCKS**!

VOCABULARY

A PAIR OF: UM PAR DE.
BOOTS: BOTAS.
CLOTHES: ROUPAS.
COAT: CASACO.
DRESS: VESTIDO.
PANTS: CALÇA.
SHIRT: CAMISA.
SHOES: SAPATOS.
SOCKS: MEIAS.
T-SHIRT: CAMISETA.

COMPREHENSION

1 WHO ARE THE GIRLS IN THE STORY?

☐ ANNE.   ☐ JUDY.   ☐ MEGAN.   ☐ AVA.

2 WHAT ARE THEY TALKING ABOUT?

_____

3 WHAT SHOULD ANNE WEAR? COLOR THE CORRECT ITEMS.

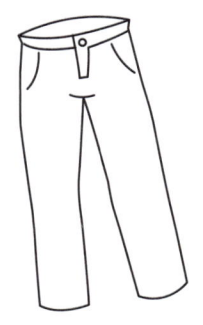

PANTS

SKIRT

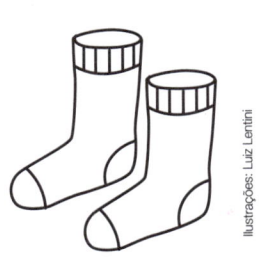

SOCKS

T-SHIRT

SHOES

FLIP-FLOPS

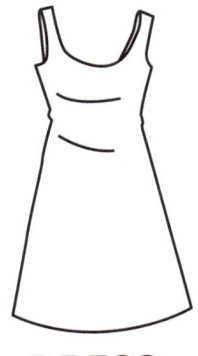

DRESS

COAT

SNEAKERS

NINETY-FIVE **95**

LET'S PLAY

1 LISTEN, NUMBER, AND COLOR.

☐ UNDERWEAR

☐ SOCKS

☐ SKIRT

☐ SHIRT

☐ PANTS

☐ SHORTS

☐ COAT

☐ DRESS

☐ PAJAMAS

☐ BOOTS

☐ SNEAKERS

☐ SHOES

☐ FLIP-FLOPS

2 WHAT IS THIS? PASTE THE STICKERS AND WRITE.

A) IT IS A _____.

C) IT IS A _____.

B) IT IS A _____.

D) IT IS A _____.

HOKEY-POKEY

YOU **PUT** YOUR RIGHT **FOOT** IN,
YOU PUT YOUR **RIGHT** FOOT **OUT**,
AND YOU **SHAKE** IT ALL ABOUT!
YOU DO THE HOKEY-POKEY,
AND YOU **TURN YOURSELF AROUND**.
YOU PUT YOUR **LEFT** FOOT IN,
YOU PUT YOUR LEFT FOOT OUT,
AND YOU SHAKE IT ALL ABOUT!
YOU DO THE HOKEY-POKEY,
AND YOU TURN YOURSELF AROUND.
YOU PUT YOUR RIGHT **HAND** IN,
YOU PUT YOUR RIGHT HAND OUT,
AND YOU SHAKE IT ALL ABOUT!
YOU DO THE HOKEY-POKEY,

VOCABULARY

FOOT: PÉ.
HAND: MÃO.
HEAD: CABEÇA.
IN: DENTRO.
LEFT: ESQUERDO(A).
OUT: FORA.
PUT (TO PUT): COLOCA (COLOCAR).
RIGHT: DIREITO(A).
SHAKE (TO SHAKE): SACODE (SACUDIR).
TURN AROUND (TO TURN AROUND): VIRA/GIRA (VIRAR/GIRAR).
WHOLE: INTEIRO(A).
YOURSELF: VOCÊ MESMO(A).

Vanessa Alexandre

LET'S SING!

AND YOU TURN YOURSELF AROUND.
YOU PUT YOUR LEFT HAND IN,
YOU PUT YOUR LEFT HAND OUT,
AND YOU SHAKE IT ALL ABOUT!
YOU DO THE HOKEY-POKEY,
AND YOU TURN YOURSELF AROUND.
YOU PUT YOUR **HEAD IN**,
YOU PUT YOUR HEAD OUT,
AND YOU SHAKE IT ALL ABOUT!
YOU DO THE HOKEY-POKEY,
AND YOU TURN YOURSELF AROUND.
YOU PUT YOUR **WHOLE** SELF IN,
YOU PUT YOUR WHOLE SELF OUT,
AND YOU SHAKE IT ALL ABOUT!
YOU DO THE HOKEY-POKEY,
AND YOU TURN YOURSELF AROUND.

POPULAR SONG.

GRAMMAR POINT

SUBJECT PRONOUN

IT (ELE/ELA PARA COISAS, OBJETOS E ANIMAIS)

THE COAT IS BLUE.

IT IS BLUE.

THE SKIRT IS GREEN.

IT IS GREEN.

LET'S PLAY

1 USE THE CORRECT PRONOUN: **HE**, **SHE**, OR **IT**.

A) THE GIRL WEARS A DRESS.
_____ WEARS A DRESS.

B) THE BOY PLAYS SOCCER.
_____ PLAYS SOCCER.

C) THE DOG IS BIG AND DOCILE.
_____ IS BIG AND DOCILE.

2 COLOR THE CORRECT PRONOUN: **HE**, **SHE**, OR **IT**.

A) HE SHE IT

B) HE SHE IT

C) HE SHE IT

D) HE SHE IT

GOOD DEED

CLOTHES FOR DONATION!
LET'S DO A DONATION CAMPAIGN.

LET'S LISTEN

1 LISTEN AND COMPLETE.

A) TERRY WEARS A RED T-SHIRT AND A RED PAIR OF SNEAKERS.
THE _____ IS RED. IT ___ RED.
THE PAIR OF _____ IS RED. IT ___ RED.

B) KATE HAS A BIG DOG AND A SMALL CAT.
THE _____ IS BIG. IT ___ BIG.
THE _____ IS SMALL. IT ___ SMALL.

ENGLISH AROUND THE WORLD

CLOTHING AROUND THE WORLD

KOREAN GIRL WEARING A TRADITIONAL *HANBOK*.

LITTLE GIRL DRESSED IN TRADITIONAL INDIAN *SARI* TO CELEBRATE INDIAN FESTIVALS.

SCOTTISH BOY DRESSING A *KILT*.

BOY DRESSED IN TRADITIONAL GAÚCHA CLOTHES.

LET'S HAVE FUN

1 WHICH SOCK HAS NO PAIR? FIND IT AND CIRCLE.

DIGITAL PLAY

LET'S PLAY AN ONLINE MEMORY GAME!

AFTER THIS UNIT I CAN

IDENTIFY AND NAME DIFFERENT PIECES OF CLOTHING.

REFLECT ON THE USE OF CLOTHING AND SUSTAINABILITY.

DESCRIBE MY FAVORITE CLOTHES.

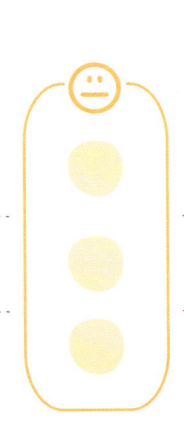

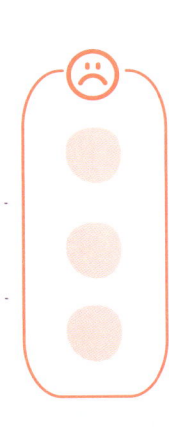

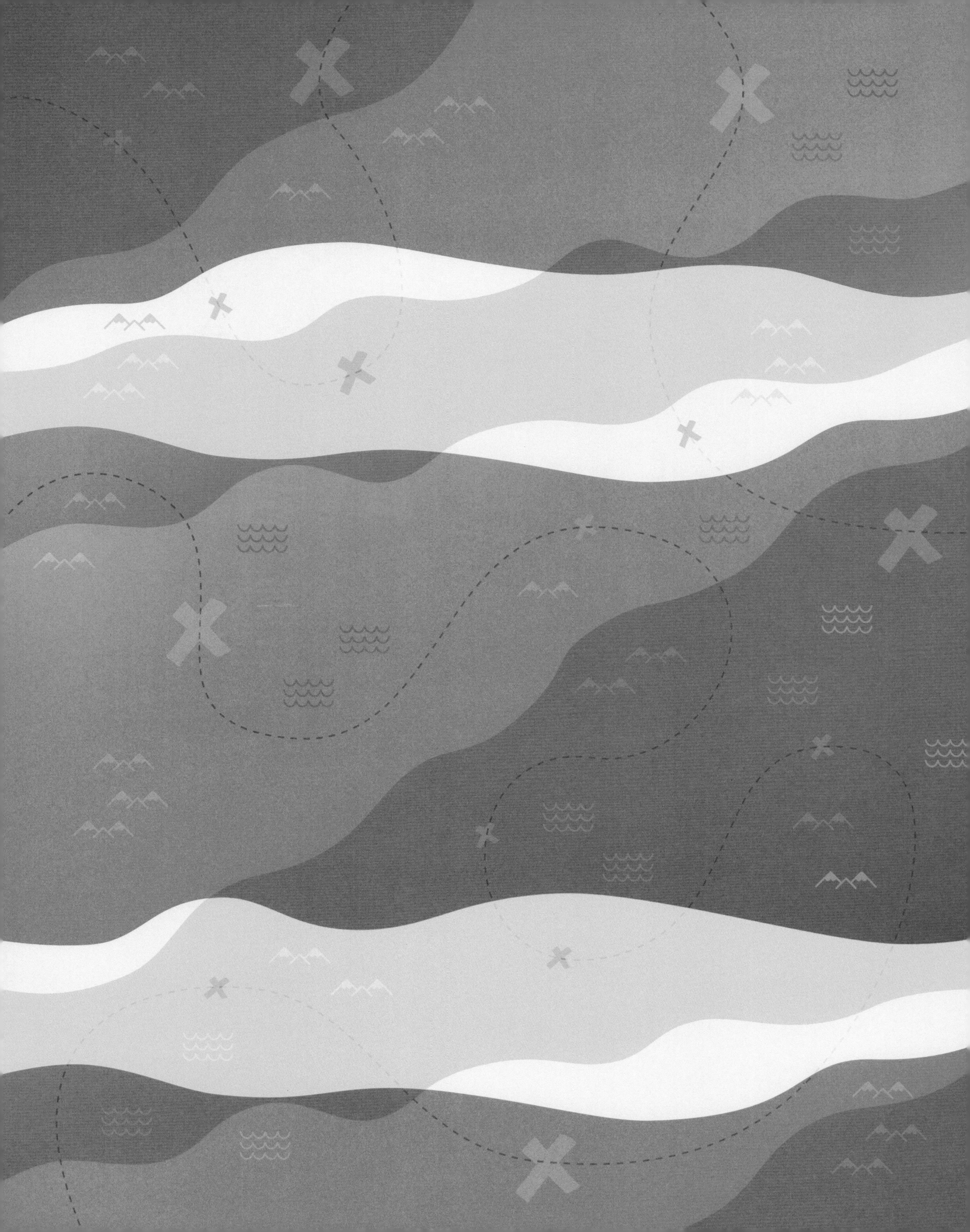

REVIEW

UNIT 1

1 WHAT DO THEY LIKE TO PLAY? LOOK AT THE PICTURES AND WRITE.

A) _____

B) _____

2 LOOK AT THE PICTURES AND CHECK THE CORRECT OPTION.

- ☐ GOOD MORNING!
- ☐ GOOD EVENING!

- ☐ HELLO! NICE TO MEET YOU.
- ☐ GOOD NIGHT!

ONE HUNDRED SEVEN 107

UNIT 2

1 HOW MANY? COUNT THE CATS AND WRITE THE NUMBERS.

2 GUESS THE ANIMAL. THEN WRITE.

UNIT 3

1 LOOK AT THE IMAGES AND COMPLETE THE CROSSWORD PUZZLE.

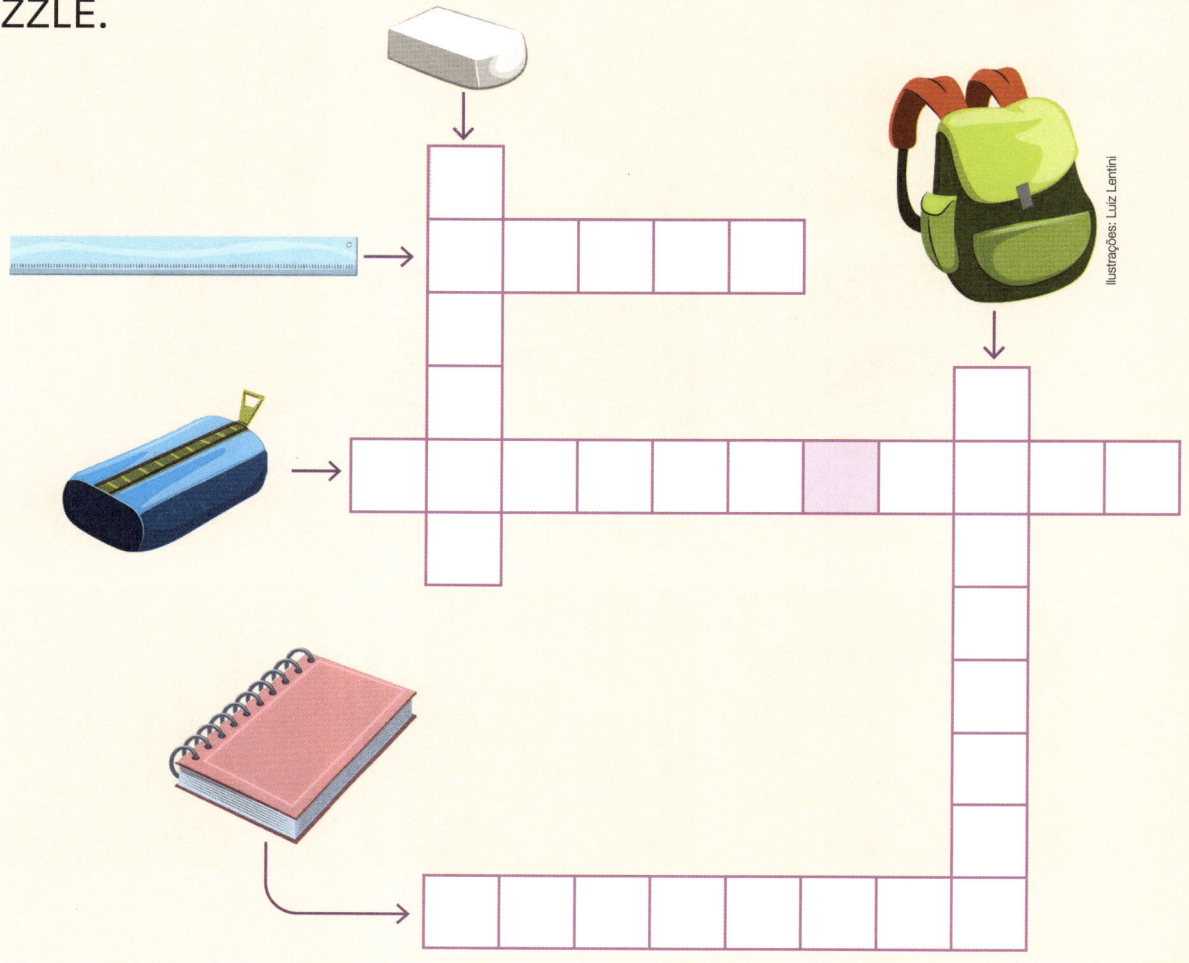

2 COLOR THE LETTERS OF YOUR NAME.

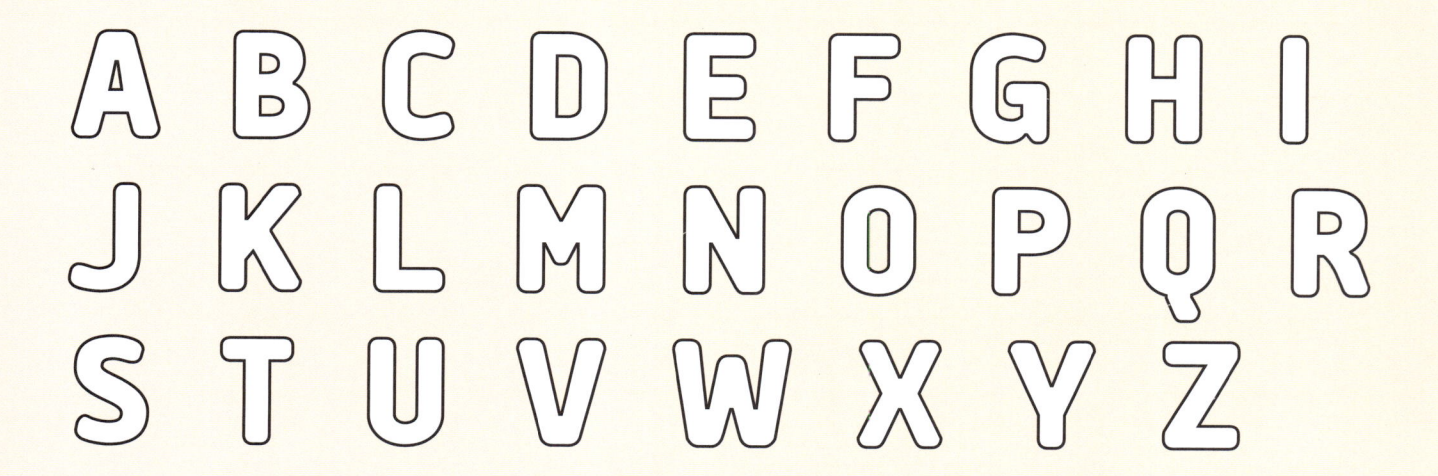

A B C D E F G H I
J K L M N O P Q R
S T U V W X Y Z

3 COLOR THE NUMBERS AND ITS NAME WITH THE SAME COLOR.

14 ONE 5 NINE 10
7 TWO 11 TEN 13
THREE ELEVEN
3 6
FOUR TWELVE
1 8
FIVE THIRTEEN
12 SIX 4 FOURTEEN
SEVEN FIFTEEN
15 EIGHT 2 9

ONE HUNDRED ELEVEN

UNIT 4

1 FIND THE WORDS, CIRCLE, AND COLOR THE DESSERTS.

```
B S P R E A I C E   C R E A M A
T S N S O R R A C N E A P L I O
G A E A P I N E A P P L E V K L
C O O F T X E Q R V S   A R L N
D C A P E A R E N A N A N H O R
O A B U E H E M S L I M E S I Z
I W B A N A N A B N H I O T P R
Y O A P L C C R E N A P P L E T
```

112 ONE HUNDRED TWELVE

UNIT 5

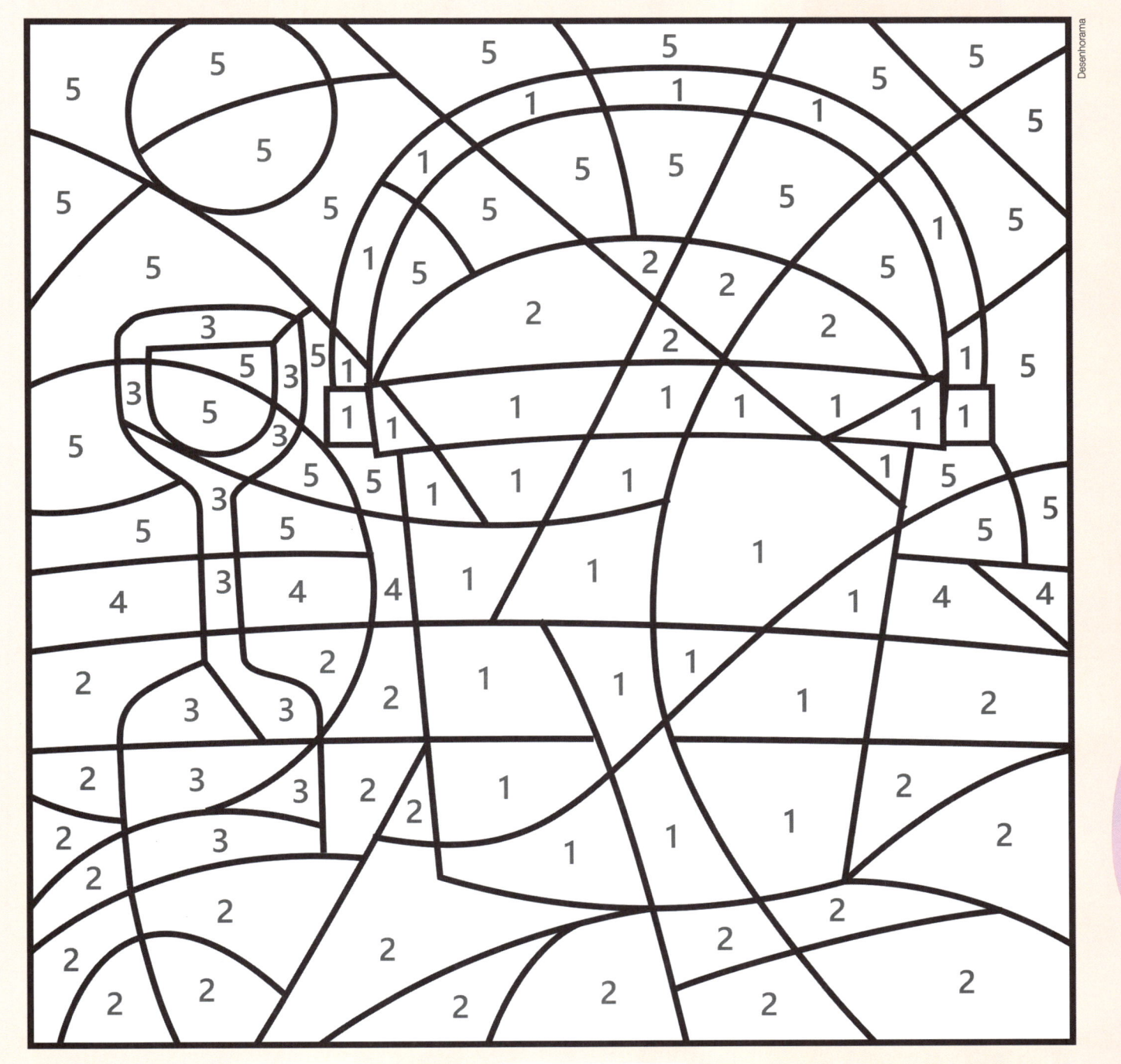

1 LOOK AND COLOR. THEN WRITE WHAT IT IS.

1 2 3 4 5

IT'S A _____ AND A _____.

2 LOOK AT THE IMAGES AND COMPLETE THE MISSING LETTER.

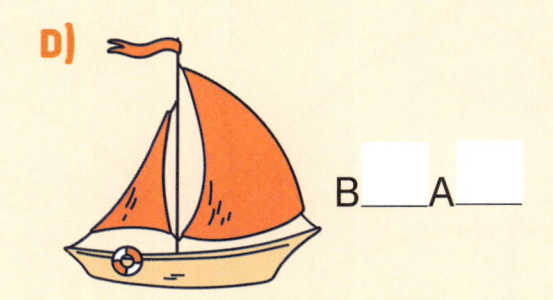

A) SU___

B) PA___ASO___

C) ___ALL

D) B___A___

3 FIND THE 10 DIFFERENCES AND COLOR THE IMAGES.

UNIT 6

1 DRAW YOUR FAMILY.

2 NUMBER THE MEMBERS OF THE FAMILY.

1. FATHER
2. MOTHER
3. SON
4. DAUGHTER
5. GRANDMOTHER
6. GRANDFATHER
7. UNCLE
8. AUNT
9. COUSIN

UNIT 7

1 FIND AND CIRCLE THE OBJECTS IN THE WORDSEARCH PUZZLE.

SOFA

SINK

BOOKCASE

STOVE

SHOWER

TOILET SEAT

REFRIGERATOR

T	O	I	L	E	T	S	E	A	T	H	K
S	D	F	H	J	W	T	U	N	M	X	D	K
C	R	E	F	R	I	G	E	R	A	T	O	R
U	D	B	O	O	K	C	A	S	E	O	P	A
H	E	F	B	N	G	R	H	M	K	Y	U
B	S	S	H	O	W	E	R	X	Z	Q	I	O
D	S	I	N	K	M	L	P	F	W	E	S	H
F	C	N	G	B	V	D	S	O	F	A	G	H
R	Y	L	E	B	I	Y	M	S	T	O	V	E
D	J	B	N	M	E	Q	A	H	X	S	K	L

UNIT 8

1 WRITE THE NAMES OF THE CLOTHING ITEMS.

A)  IT IS A _____.

B)  IT IS A _____.

C)  IT IS A _____.

D)  IT IS A _____.

E)  IT IS A PAIR OF _____.

F)  IT IS A PAIR OF _____.

PICTURE DICTIONARY

A

APPLE

ARMCHAIR

BED

BEDSIDE TABLE

BLOUSE

BOAT

B

BATHTUB

BEACH

BEANS

BEET

BIRD

BLACK

BOOKCASE

BREAD

BREAKFAST

BROTHER

BUCKET

BUILDING

BUTTER

C

CAKE

CAMPSITE

CANDY

CAR

CARROT

CAT

CHEESE

CHIMNEY

CLOTHES

COAT

ONE HUNDRED NINETEEN 119

COFFEE

COUNTRYSIDE

CUPBOARD

D

DESK

DOG

DRESS

E

ELEPHANT

ERASER

F

FAMILY

FATHER

FISH

FLIP-FLOPS

FOOD

FRUIT SALAD

FURNITURE

G

GRANDMOTHER / GRANDFATHER

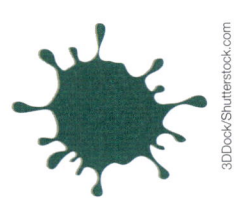

GREEN

GUINEA PIG

H

HAMBURGER

HAMSTER

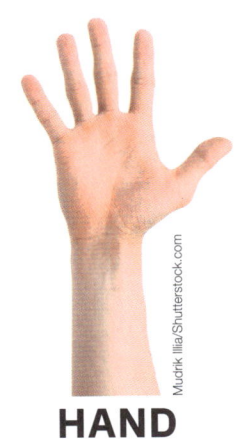

HAND

HEAD

HORSE

HOUSE

I

ICE CREAM

J

JUICE

K

KITCHEN

L

LAKE

LAMP

LION

LIVING ROOM

M

MEAT

MICROWAVE OVEN

MIRROR

MOTHER

MOVIE

O

ORANGE

P

PAJAMAS

PAN

PANTS

PARASOL

PASTA

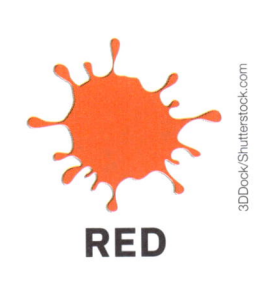

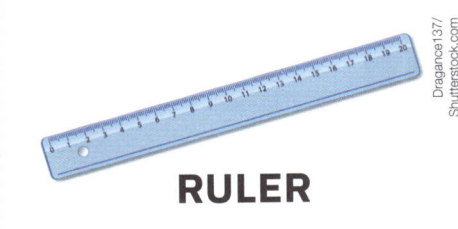

PEACH

PEN

PENCIL

R

RABBIT

RECTANGLE

RED

REFRIGERATOR

RICE

RIVER

ROOF

RUG

RULER

S

SAILOR

SALAD

SANDWICH

ONE HUNDRED TWENTY-THREE 123

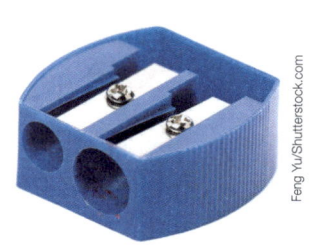

SCHOOL	**SHIRT**	**SISTER**
SEA	**SHOES**	**SKIRT**
SHARPENER	**SHOVEL**	**SKY**
SHEEP	**SHOWER**	**SNEAKERS**
SHELF	**SINK**	**SOAP**

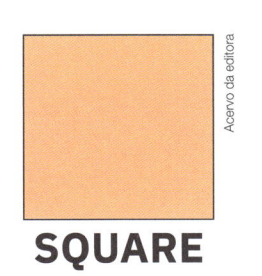

SOCKS	**STREET**	**TEACHER**
SODA	**STUDENT**	**TIGER**
SQUARE	**SUN**	**TOILET SEAT**
	SWING	**TOWEL**
STOVE	**T-SHIRT**	**TOY**

ONE HUNDRED TWENTY-FIVE 125

TREE

TRIANGLE

TURTLE

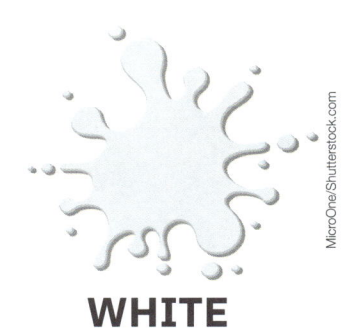

W

WARDROBE

Y

WHITE

YELLOW

YOGURT

126 ONE HUNDRED TWENTY-SIX

INDEX

SONGS

UNIT 1 THE GOOD MORNING TRAIN IS COMING 24
UNIT 2 FISH STORY 32
UNIT 3 HELLO, HELLO, HELLO 44
UNIT 4 FIVE FAT SAUSAGES 55
UNIT 5 A SAILOR WENT TO SEA, SEA, SEA 64
UNIT 6 THE FAMILY 76
UNIT 7 THAT IS MY HOUSE 90
UNIT 8 HOKEY-POKEY 98

LISTENINGS

UNIT 1
- FUN TIME WITH FRIENDS 15
- WHAT ARE THEY SAYING? LISTEN AND NUMBER 21

UNIT 2
- I LOVE PETS 27
- LISTEN AND COLOR THE CORRECT WORD 33

UNIT 3
- A SPECIAL PLACE, THE SCHOOL! 36
- LISTEN, REPEAT, AND COLOR 39
- HOW MANY? LISTEN, CIRCLE, AND WRITE 46

UNIT 4
- MY FAVORITE FOOD 48
- LISTEN, REPEAT, AND CIRCLE 50
- LISTEN, ANSWER, AND COLOR 53

UNIT 5
- SUMMER VACATIONS 58
- WHERE DO YOU WANT TO SPEND YOUR SUMMER VACATION? 68

UNIT 6
- OUR FAMILY 69
- LISTEN AND REPEAT. THEN COLOR THE CHILDREN 72
- LISTEN AND PASTE THE STICKERS IN THE CORRECT COLUMN 73

UNIT 7
- HOME SWEET HOME 81
- WHAT'S IN THE KITCHEN? LISTEN AND NUMBER THE OBJECTS 85
- WHAT'S IN THE LIVING ROOM? LISTEN AND PASTE THE STICKERS. 86

UNIT 8
- MY CLOTHES 94
- LISTEN, NUMBER, AND COLOR 96
- LISTEN AND COMPLETE 102

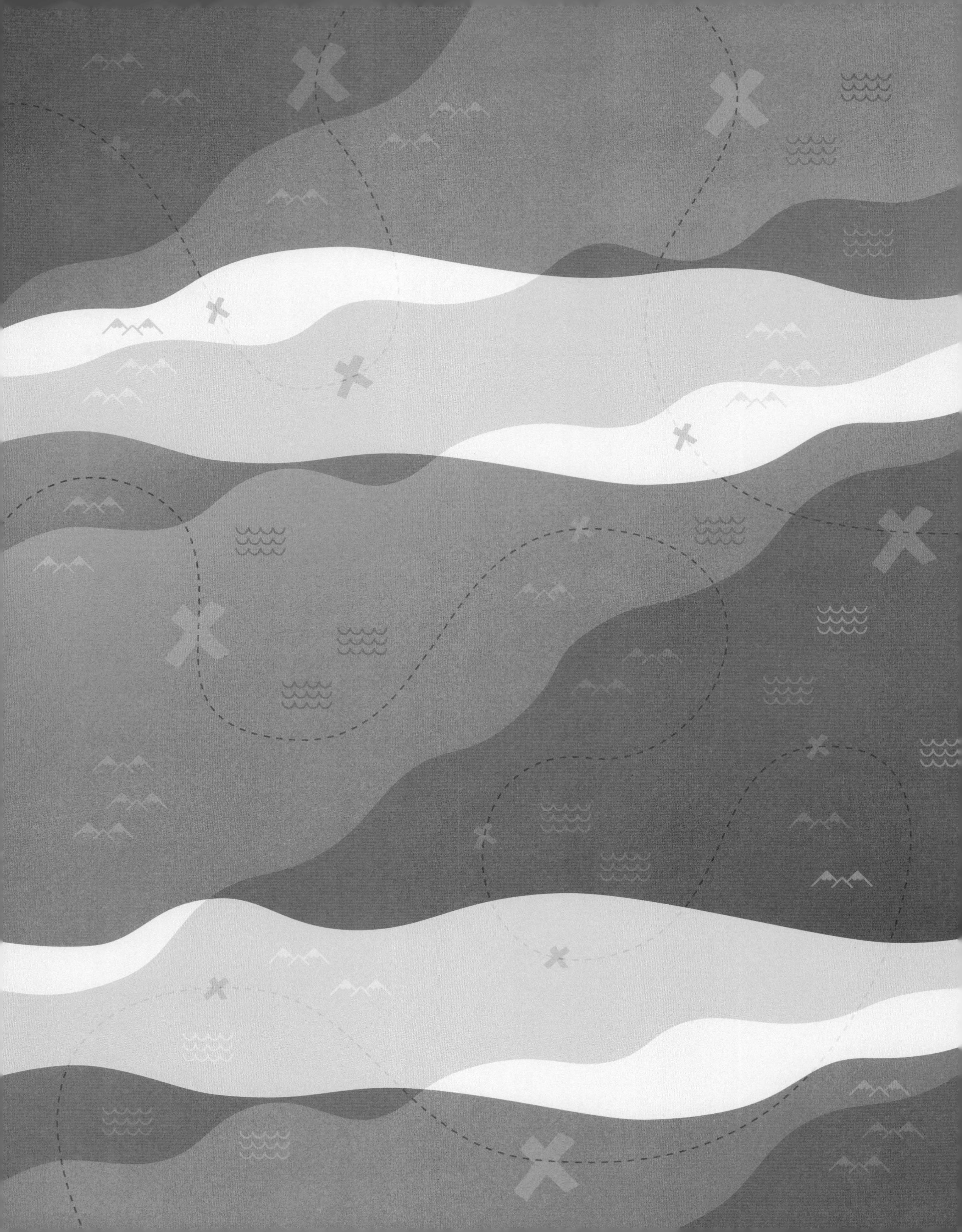

CELEBRATIONS

VALENTINE'S DAY

EASTER

EASTER
EGG HUNT

WORLD ENVIRONMENT DAY

INTERNATIONAL FAMILY'S DAY

137

THANKSGIVING DAY

CHRISTMAS

CHRISTMAS

LET'S START
PAGE 8

STICKERS

UNIT 1
PAGE 18

STICKERS

UNIT 2
PAGE 28

PAGE 35

UNIT 3
PAGE 40

ONE HUNDRED FORTY-SEVEN 147

STICKERS

UNIT 4
PAGE 49

PAGE 57

UNIT 6
PAGE 73

MARY    KATE    JENNY

STICKERS

SCOTT    EDWARD    TOMMY

UNIT 7
PAGE 86

UNIT 8
PAGE 97

ONE HUNDRED FIFTY-ONE **151**

MY ALPHABET

Ilustrações © Rodrigo Cordeiro

© Editora do Brasil S.A., 2024
Todos os direitos reservados

Direção-geral	Paulo Serino de Souza
Direção editorial	Felipe Ramos Poletti
Gerência editorial de produção e design	Ulisses Pires
Supervisão editorial	Carla Felix Lopes e Diego da Mata
Edição	Camile Mendrot | Ab Aeterno
Assistência editorial	Marcos Vasconcelos e Pedro Andrade Bezerra; Enrico Payão | Ab Aeterno
Auxílio editorial	Natalia Soeda
Supervisão de arte	Abdonildo José de Lima Santos
Edição de arte e diagramação	Ana Clara Suzano | Ab Aeterno
Design gráfico	Ariane Adriele O. Costa
Supervisão de revisão	Elaine Cristina da Silva
Revisão	Natasha Greenhouse e Sarah Garnett | Ab Aeterno

1ª edição / 1ª impressão, 2024
Impresso na Hawaii Gráfica e Editora

Editora do Brasil

Avenida das Nações Unidas, 12901
Torre Oeste, 20º andar
São Paulo, SP – CEP: 04578-910
www.editoradobrasil.com.br

abdr — ASSOCIAÇÃO BRASILEIRA DOS DIREITOS REPROGRÁFICOS
Respeite o direito autoral

MY ALPHABET

MARIA CAROLINA RODRIGUES
ILUSTRAÇÕES: RODRIGO CORDEIRO

Editora do Brasil

A IS FOR AMY. AMY IS MY SISTER.

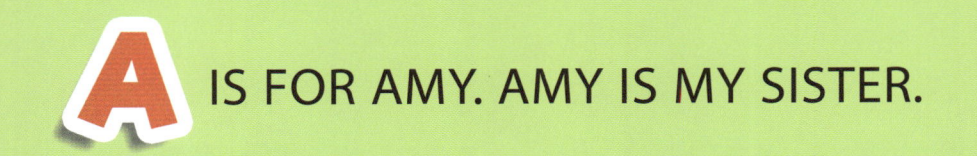

B IS FOR BEN. BEN IS MY BROTHER.

C IS FOR CAROL. CAROL IS MY MOTHER.

D IS FOR DAVID. DAVID IS MY FATHER.

E IS FOR ELSA AND ELLIOT.

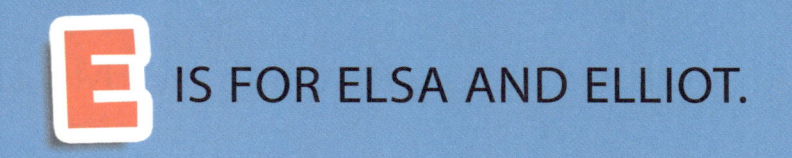

ELSA IS MY GRANDMOTHER AND ELLIOT IS MY GRANDFATHER.

F IS FOR FAMILY.

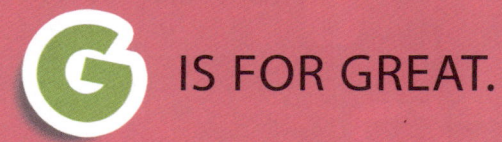

G IS FOR GREAT.

H IS FOR HAPPY.

I LIKE MY GREAT HAPPY FAMILY!

I IS FOR IVY.

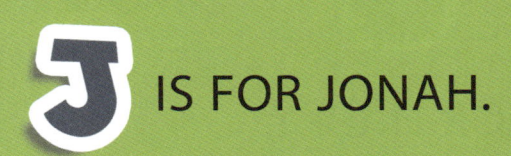

J IS FOR JONAH.

IVY AND JONAH ARE MY FRIENDS!

K IS FOR KATE. KATE IS MY AUNT.

L IS FOR LOVE.

I LOVE TO PLAY WITH MY AUNT KATE!

M IS FOR MARK. MARK IS MY UNCLE.

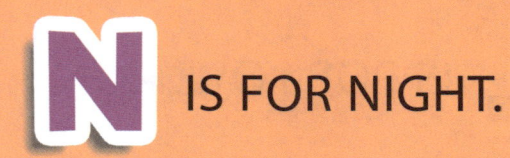

N IS FOR NIGHT.

I READ BOOKS WITH MY UNCLE MIKE AT NIGHT!

O IS FOR ORANGE. ORANGE IS MY FAVORITE COLOR.

P IS FOR PASTA. PASTA IS MY FAVORITE FOOD.

I EAT MY PASTA ON AN ORANGE PLATE!

Q IS FOR QUIET.

R IS FOR RABBIT.

MY PET RABBIT IS ALWAYS VERY, VERY QUIET.

S IS FOR SCHOOL.

T IS FOR TEACHER.

I LEARN A LOT AT SCHOOL WITH MY TEACHER, MISS HONEY.

U IS FOR URSULA. URSULA IS MY NEIGHBOR.

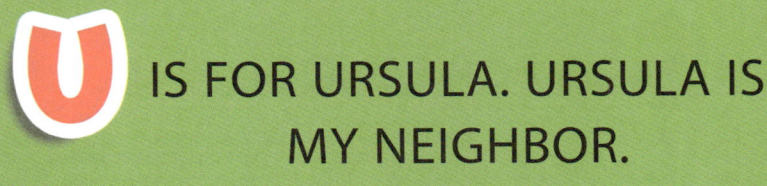

V IS FOR VEGETABLE.

URSULA HAS A VEGETABLE GARDEN.

W IS FOR WHAT.

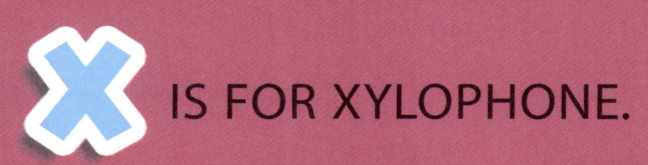

X IS FOR XYLOPHONE.

WHAT IS A XYLOPHONE?
I STILL HAVE TO LEARN.

Y IS FOR YELLOW. YELLOW LIKE THE COLOR OF MY DRESS.

AND **Z** IS FOR ZOE. THAT'S MY NAME!